Good Luck Dave

Mrs Patricia Bresnahan
3 Wesite Ave
Dundas ON L9H 5M1

Case

HISTORY OF THE

ROYAL CANADIAN AIR FORCE

HISTORY OF THE

⊙ROYAL⊙
CANADIAN
AIR FORCE

Christopher Shores

Royce Publications
Toronto, Canada

A BISON BOOK

Published in 1984 by
Royce Publications
Toronto, Canada

Produced by
Bison Books Corp
17 Sherwood Place
Greenwich, CT 06830
USA

ISBN 0 86124 160 6

Printed in Hong Kong

CONTENTS

THE BIRTH OF CANADIAN MILITARY AVIATION

Although the land mass of Canada covers a vast area of North America and encompasses untold natural wealth it is a small nation in terms of population. In consequence the contribution of Canada and her citizens to the history of military aviation has been quite unique. Despite limited resources of both people and finance, Canadian involvement in World Wars I and II, and in the North Atlantic Treaty Organization since that time, has been generous and unselfish in the extreme.

It was in 1908 that the first experimental aeroplane was built in Canada – J A D McCurdy's 'Silver Dart'. Douglas McCurdy, aided by 'Casey' Baldwin, Glenn Curtiss and Lt Selfridge of the US Army, constructed the machine, which he first flew on 23 February 1909. Flights in 'Silver Dart' were increased in height and distance until 20 miles at a time were being covered, and before long the little aircraft had covered nearly 1000 miles in the air. Attempts to interest the military authorities came to nothing, however, when Baldwin crashed the aircraft before the eyes of the skeptical and conservative Army officers.

There were those who saw the potential, however, but lack of funds precluded any acquisitions until the outbreak of war in Europe in August 1914. Anxious not to be 'out of the swim', the military then authorized the purchase of a single Burgess-Dunne biplane in the United States, and in October this and two officers formed the basis of the grandly-named Canadian Aviation Corps, which was despatched with the Canadian Expeditionary Force to Britain. Here the sole example of the type available, the aircraft sat unused on Salisbury Plain, deteriorating until it was finally scrapped. As no further equipment or personnel were forthcoming, the commander returned to Canada where he resigned his appointment. The other officer, Lt W F Sharpe, remained in England where he was killed in a flying accident in a Royal Flying Corps aircraft on 4 February 1915.

It was to be in men rather than machines or organization that Canada was to make her main contribution to the first war in the air.

Initially, these came from two sources; disillusioned members of the Expeditionary Force in France, seeing the war on the ground bogged down in the morass of the trenches, volunteered to join the Royal Flying Corps in order to escape the depersonalized, abject conditions and to make a more individual contribution to the fighting in the new medium above. However, with young men flocking to join the Army, Canada also proved a fruitful ground for direct recruitment by the fledgling Royal Naval Air Service. Many young men had attempted to join the British flying services, but had been turned down initially because they could not fly. It was intimated, however, that if they could obtain pilot's certificates, they would at once be accepted by the RNAS. In September 1915 a Curtiss School of aviation was set up at Long Branch, Ontario, and it was here, or at schools in the United States, that most young hopefuls went. Indeed the Curtiss school, with its five Curtiss JN-3 trainers and three flying boats was overwhelmed with over 1000 applicants.

The first Canadians were soon in service and at the front, and on 14 December 1915 Flight Sub Lt Arthur Strachan Ince, observer to Flt Sub Lt C W Graham, shot down a German seaplane off the coast of Belgium, the first Canadian aerial victory, for which he was awarded the first decoration to go to a Canadian for air fighting – a Distinguished Service Cross.

The first Canadian Naval airman to see action was in fact Flt Sub Lt Redford H Mulock. Not a recruit in Canada, Mulock had served with the Field Artillery since 1911, transferring to the RNAS in 1915. Based at Dunkirk with 1 Wing from July 1915 onwards, he was soon in action against aircraft, submarines and shipping, and on 30 December of that year he drove down a German aircraft in a steep dive near Dixmude. During early 1916 he was to drive two more aircraft down out of control, and drive off four more during the summer while on escort operations. While these victories were almost entirely of a moral, rather than physical nature, they were important in the context of his duties, and in June 1916 he was awarded a Distinguished Service Order, to which he later gained a

Bar, or second award. In 1917 he commanded one of the new RNAS fighting scout squadrons at the front – a most respected and experienced leader and pilot.

Meanwhile the products of the new recruitment were arriving, and in summer 1916 the RNAS's first offensive unit was formed for service in France. 3 (Naval) Wing was equipped with Sopwith 1½ Strutter two-seaters, mainly for bombing, and the personnel of the Wing included 40 Canadians, many of them future notables such as Raymond Collishaw, J E Sharman, W M Alexander, A T Whealey, A W Carter, S T Edwards, E V Reid, J J Malone, J A Glen, F C Armstrong, G E Nash and J S T Fall, all of whom were destined to become leading Naval fighter 'aces'.

The first Canadian 'ace' was to be Flt Lt Edward R Grange, however. By late 1916 naval fighting squadrons, equipped initially with Nieuports and Sopwith Pups, were coming into service to operate in defense of the naval bases at Dunkirk and along the Franco-Belgian coast. One of the first graduates of the Curtiss School, Grange served with 1 (Naval) Squadron, seeing his first combats in August and November 1916. During January 1917 he claimed five aircraft shot down out of control in four days, three of them on the 4th. Wounded in the shoulder during his final combat on the 7th, he was subsequently awarded a DSC, but saw no further action.

In the spring of 1917 the RFC was hard-pressed by the German fighting scouts, and was short of good modern fighting aircraft, and of pilots to fly them. To fill the gap the RNAS offered fighting squadrons for service alongside the RFC on the Western Front – an offer that was gratefully accepted. Initially the Pup squadrons at Dunkirk were thrown into the line, but at the same time 3 Wing was disbanded to provide pilots for new units just as supplies of the excellent Sopwith Triplane scout became available. Soon 1, 3, 8, 9 and 10 Squadrons were active over the front, joined later in the summer by 4 and 6 Squadrons with the first of the new Sopwith Camels.

**Previous pages: Senior personnel of 1 and 2 Squadrons, Canadian Air Force, with their Sopwith Dolphins in 1918. On the left is Capt. D R MacLaren DSO, MC★, DFC (54 victories flying Camels), while next to him is the O C of 1 Squadron, Maj A E McKeever DSO, MC★, top-scoring Bristol Fighter pilot of WWI with 30 victories.
Above: W G Barker, the Third Canadian VC of World War I, prepares to take off in his famous Camel, B6313, while serving as a Captain with 28 Squadron, RFC. B6313 was the top-scoring Camel of the war.
Below: Canada provided a base for RFC training during World War I, though all Canadian military aviation was controlled by the British service. Locally-built Curtiss JN-4 trainers of Royal Flying Corps, Canada, are seen here ready for a day's work.**

Among the most notable of these naval pilots were Canadians J Stuart Fall, Ray Collishaw and A T Whealy. Collishaw commanded a flight in 10 Squadron comprising five Canadians – himself, Sharman, Reid, Nash and Alexander – which claimed 87 victories in the three months May-July 1917, 33 of them by Collishaw and 18 each by Alexander and Reid. Many of the great RNAS pilots continued to command old Naval squadrons during 1918 after the RNAS and RFC had been amalgamated to form the new Royal Air Force, and when the war ended Collishaw was the highest-scoring of these with 60 victories – the third highest total of all British Empire pilots. Four other Canadian naval pilots had scores in excess of 20; Fall was credited with 34 – all claimed during 1917 flying Pups and Camels; Whealy had 27, gained on Pups, Triplanes and Camels between April 1917 and August 1918, while Stanley Rosevear had 23 and Charles Hickey 21. Both Rosevear and Hickey were killed in flying accidents before the end of the war. Some 36 more Canadian naval pilots became aces, five of them with scores between 15 and 19. Some were later to see high service; Collishaw became an Air Vice-Marshal in the RAF, while Lloyd S Breadner (10 victories) joined the new Canadian Air Force after the war, becoming Chief of Air Staff of the RCAF in 1940 with the rank of Air Chief Marshal. This post was held in 1947 by Air Marshal W A Curtis, who had claimed 13 victories flying Camels with 6 and 10 Squadrons between September 1917 and January 1918.

While the RNAS pilots had done well, so too had many of those Canadians who had joined the RFC after service in France, and others who later joined that service or the RAF direct from home. Among the original transferees, Maj W A Bishop had become RFC top-scorer by the middle of August 1917 with 45 victories. He was also the first Canadian airman to be awarded a Victoria Cross for a single-handed dawn attack on a German airfield on 2 June. He later returned to France to command an SE 5A unit, 85 Squadron, adding 27 more victories to raise his total to 72 and regain his premier position. He also subsequently held senior rank in the RCAF.

After service as a reconnaissance pilot, Maj W G Barker became a Camel flyer, but after gaining seven victories over the Western Front, he was posted with his squadron to Italy. Here he quickly established himself as the leading RFC scout pilot, claiming 42 victories against the Austro-Hungarians between November 1917

and September 1918. Posted back to Britain as an instructor, he managed to get back to France with one of the new Sopwith Snipe fighters in October 1918. There he became involved in an epic dogfight on 27 October when against a swarm of Fokker D.VIII scouts, he was seen to shoot down three after first despatching a two-seater, before he was shot down and badly wounded himself. He too received a Victoria Cross.

Barker's score of 53 was just topped by another Canadian Camel pilot, Maj D R MacLaren. One of those joining the RFC directly from home, MacLaren served with 46 Squadron on the Western Front throughout 1918, being credited with 54 victories. Canada also produced the two top-scoring two-seater pilots. Another of the early transferees, Capt Andrew E McKeever claimed 30 victories flying Bristol Fighters with 11 Squadron during the summer and fall of 1917. After his departure from the front, Lt A C Atkey, who had gained four victories flying DH-4 bombers, was transferred to 22 Squadron to fly Bristol Fighters, claiming 29 more successes in just one month, 7 May-2 June 1918.

Altogether 12 Canadians gained 20 or more victories with the RFC and its derivative RAF units, the others including Capt William Claxton (36) who flew SE 5As with 41 Squadron during 1918, and Capt Frederick McCall who gained most of his 37 victories in the same unit; Maj. A. D. 'Nick' Carter flew Spads and Sopwith Dolphins with 19 Squadrons, claiming 31 victories, while like Barker, Lt C M MacEwen flew Camels in Italy, gaining 27 victories there. French-based Camel pilots Captains Francis Quigley (25) and J M White (22) flew with 70 and 65 Squadrons respectively, while Capt W E Shields (20) was yet another 41 Squadron SE 5A pilot. All but one of these pilots survived the war, though Claxton and Carter had both become prisoners of war, the former with severe head wounds. Quigley was the exception – and he died of influenza in October 1918 while returning to France after a period spent as an instructor at home.

Nine more Canadians claimed between 15 and 19 victories with the RFC/RAF, and 26 more claimed at least ten out of a total of 111 who became 'aces'. In all during the war at least 152 Canadian scout pilots claimed five or more victories – about 13 percent of all Empire pilots to do so. Among the top scorers, of nine pilots with scores above 50, four were Canadians, who received two of the five Victoria

Above right: Official British Empire top-scoring scout pilot of World War I was Maj W A 'Billy' Bishop VC, DSO, MC, DFC. The Canadian ace is seen here (right) on the day he left 85 Squadron RAF, following his 72nd victory.
Below: The first Canadian Air Force unit, 1 Squadron, was formed by renumbering 81 Squadron, RAF, in November 1918 – just too late to see action over the front. Eight of the unit's Sopwith Dolphins are seen here at Upper Heyford, England.

Above: Canadian top-scorer of the Royal Naval Air Service was Maj Ray Collishaw DSO★, DFC, seen here in early 1918 when commanding 3 (Naval) Squadron in France. With 60 victories, Collishaw was third among Empire top-scorers.

Crosses awarded to this group. One Canadian Corps reconnaissance pilot was also awarded the VC, while 203 Canadians received the new Distinguished Flying Cross medal instituted after the formation of the RAF in April 1918; nine received Bars to this medal. Altogether Canadian airmen received over 800 decorations during the war; some 22,000 men from the Dominion served with the British air forces, of whom 1,563 lost their lives.

In Canada meanwhile the Canadian-Curtiss Aeroplane and Motors Company Ltd had been formed in March 1915, producing JN-3 trainers for the RNAS and flying boats for the Imperial Russian forces. During December 1916 the Canadian Aeroplane Company was set up, funded by the British and Canadian governments, and this too produced Curtiss trainers – notably the JN-4 for use in Canada. The British War Office had approved the formation of 20 Canadian Reserve Squadrons (Nos 78-97) with nucleus flights to be provided from Britain, the first contingent arriving in Toronto in January 1917 under Lt Col C G Hoare to set up 'Royal Flying Corps, Canada'. Initially recruitment for the necessary ground tradesmen was undertaken, but the first JN-4s were received from the factory in February, and development of three sites began. These included Long Branch airfield (situated North of Toronto) where the Canadian Aeroplane Co products were tested; Camp

Borden – the original training base of the Expeditionary Force; and Deseronto. No 4 School of Military Aeronautics was also set up for ground training, while the necessary back-up aircraft and engine repair workshops were also organized.

In May 1917 the Canadian Reserve Squadrons were retitled Canadian Training Squadrons in line with current RFC practice, and by then training was well underway. The entry of the US into the war at this point allowed a reciprocal arrangement to be agreed. In order that training might continue during the harsh Canadian winter, a major part of the training organization would be moved south into Texas with the onset of bad weather. In return, training of US pilots would be undertaken and 180 Canadian-built JN-4s were supplied to the US Army. By October 1917, just before the move south, the organization was formed into a Brigade, with Wings as follows:

42nd Wing HQ, Camp Borden: 78, 79, 81 and 82 Canadian Training Squadrons, and the School of Aerial Gunnery
43rd Wing HQ, Deseronto: 80, 83, 84, 85, 86 and 87 Canadian Training Squadrons.
44th Wing HQ, North Toronto: 88, 89, 90, 91 and 92 Canadian Training Squadrons.

A modification of the JN-4 with a Scarff gun ring in the rear cockpit, mounting a Lewis machine gun, was developed for use by the School of Aerial Gunnery as the JN-4A. These aircraft were later also fitted with a forward-firing synchronized Vickers gun.

The 42nd and 43rd Wings, plus a new 93 CTS, moved to Texas from November 1917 to April 1918. On return the 42nd moved to Deseronto, the 43rd to North Toronto and the 44th to Camp Borden. During 1918 it was planned to switch training to Avro 504K aircraft, and pattern machines were sent over from Britain. However, production of the aircraft by Canadian Aeroplane Co only started during October, and no more than four had been built when the war came to an end on 11 November, production then being cancelled. By this time 3135 pilots and 137 observers had been trained, 2539 of whom had been sent overseas; this total does not include the US personnel who also received training from the schools.

Due to increased German U-Boat activity in the Atlantic in 1917, Admiralty requests for Canadian antisubmarine patrols had developed into the setting up of a Royal Canadian Naval Air Service. This was organized with aid from the US Navy, which initially supplied flying boats, kite balloons and personnel, the latter until Canadian replacements could be adequately trained. Four Curtiss

Above: One of three Canadian pilots to receive the Victoria Cross during WWI, 2/Lt Alan A McLeod was the only one not to fly fighting scouts. He was awarded the decoration for an action on 27 March 1918 when flying an Armstrong-Whitworth FK 8 Corps reconnaissance aircraft with 2 Squadron, RFC.
Left: Capt A Roy Brown DSC* with the Camel (B7250) which he flew in combat with the German Jagdgeschwader I on 21 April 1918 when von Richthofen went to his death.

HS-2L flying boats were operating from Baker Point, Dartmouth, and North Sydney by August 1918, and more followed. Recruitment began, but the end of the war put the whole plan in abeyance. The Americans left behind 12 HS-2Ls, 26 Liberty engines and four balloons, all of which were stored.

In Britain a Canadian Air Force was at last being set up on a similar basis to that of the Australian flying Corps. A training base was to be set up in England, and two RAF squadrons which were forming became Canadian units by arrangement with the British government. 81 Squadron, RAF, formed at Upper Heyford, Oxfordshire, with all-Canadian personnel in November 1918. Equipped with Sopwith Dolphin fighters, it was renumbered 1 Squadron, Canadian Air Force, under the command of the distinguished ex-Bristol Fighter pilot, Maj A E McKeever, DSO, MC. It was joined by 123 Squadron, similarly manned and equipped, which became 2 Squadron. The war ended before either unit could move to France or see any action, and early in 1919 both units moved to Shoreham where the Dolphins were grounded as it was intended to re-equip 1 Squadron with SE 5As and 2 Squadron with Snipes. Despite this re-equipment, the lives of both units were to be short, 1 Squadron being disbanded on 28 January 1920, and 2 Squadron a week later.

THE INTER-WAR YEARS

With the disbandment of the fledgling Canadian Air Force in the United Kingdom, Canada was left only with the residue of the now-disused training units, and the equipment of the disbanded Naval Air Service. With the euphoria of the weary peace and the hope engendered by the emergent League of Nations, the formation of an active military air force was hardly high on the list of priorities of the Dominion, but in February 1919 came an unexpected delivery of aircraft and equipment. In return for the many aircraft presented to Britain by the citizens of Canada during the war, the Overseas Club and Patriotic League now sent over a consignment for the new Canadian Air Force comprising 16 aircraft and $170,000-worth of ancilliary equipment. The aircraft included six HD-9s, one DH-9A, two Snipes, three Camels, three Dolphins and a single Avro 504K.

This small consignment was soon followed by a larger one from the government of the United Kingdom, forming part of what was known as the 'Imperial Gift' to the Dominions to form the nucleus of post war air forces – in effect a share-out between the parties of war-surplus equipment. This much larger delivery included 101 aircraft, 12 dirigible airships, six kite balloons, 14 dismantled aircraft hangars and 300 motor vehicles. The aircraft included 58 Avro 504Ks, 12 DH-4s, 12 DH-9As, 11 SE 5As, three Felixstowe F-3 and two Curtiss H-16 flying boats, two Bristol Fighters and a Snipe.

In June 1919 an Air Board was set up to control both civil and military aviation. As no establishment existed to employ the equipment so recently received, it was in large part placed in store in Halifax and Camp Borden, together with ten of the old training scheme JN-4s, while the establishment of an air force was investigated and reported upon. Following consideration, a new air force was authorized on 18 February 1920 with a provisional establishment of 1340 officers and 3905 airmen. This was, however, to be formed on a non-permanent basis, all members being part-time auxiliaries. A small Headquarters was opened in Ottawa responsible to the Air Board, and the first Air Officer Commanding, Lt Col A K Tylee, was appointed. Camp Borden was selected as the main training center as the wartime facilities still remained virtually intact. Consequently in October 1920 operations commenced here with a

series of month-long refresher courses for volunteers drawn from the huge pool of fully-trained wartime peronnel that was available. For this purpose 49 Avro 504Ks, the ten JN-4s, ten of the SE 5As and two of the Snipes, the two Bristol Fighters and six of the DH 9As were withdrawn from storage and restored to service. By March 1922 550 officers and 1272 airmen had undertaken the course, but at that point its further continuation was suspended.

Following training, aircrew began flying with units which were formed to aid the various provincial governments with such duties as forest fire patrol, aerial survey, general communications and air transport. Initially these detachments were set up at Vancouver, Morley, Winnipeg, Ottawa, Roberval and Dartmouth, and most flew the flying boats – Felixstowe F-3s and Curtiss H-16s, supplemented by the ex-Naval Air Service HS-2Ls. By 1922 it had become apparent to the Air Board that the increasingly-important role the air force was thus playing, particularly in opening up the wilderness areas of Canada, could not adequately be carried on in the long term by a purely 'part-time' force. In consequence a reorganization was started early in the year which culminated on 1 April 1924 with the reformation of a new Royal Canadian Air Force. This new organization was now a full part of the Defense Forces with a Director responsible to the Army General Staff, and was established in three major components. The first of these was the Permanent Active Air Force, which contained the regular establishment which was set at 68 officers and 307 men; in the event it was to reach only 61 and 262 before further reorganization followed. The second component was the Non Permanent Active Air Force – the continuation of the auxiliary arm which had been operating since 1920; the third component was the Reserve Air Force, a non-active body that could be called upon when necessary in times of war or national emergency.

The duties of the two active components were to continue to be mainly of a civil nature, coupled with continued training. To facilitate operations the first orders were placed during 1924 for new equipment; eight Vickers Viking IV flying boats were ordered from Vickers of England, six of which were actually to be built in

Previous pages: First new aircraft type to be ordered by the fledgling Canadian Air Force in 1924 was the Vickers Viking IV flyingboat. The first of these, F4062, is seen here being launched at Rockliffe, Ontario.
Below left: Early equipment of the Canadian Air Force included a dozen DH 9A bombers. These were used for training during the early twenties.
Below: Curtiss H 16 flyingboat – one of the earliest types supplied to the RCAF in the twenties.
Above: DH 9A F2749 in flight.
Above right: Among the aircraft taken out of storage for training purposes in 1920 were ten Curtiss JN-4s. This aircraft, fitted with a Lewis machine gun above the wing, is one of the JN-4As employed by the School of Aerial Gunnery during 1918.

Montreal. These were to be followed in 1925 by the first Canadian-built versions of the Vedette, which was developed from the Viking. Thus was the Canadian aircraft industry again set up, following its initial birth during the war years, but now on a more permanent and steadily-growing basis.

During the period 1925-7 five units formed the basis of the RCAF's operational arm, and these were as follows:

No 1 (Operations) Wing at Winnipeg with Vickers Viking, Vedette and Varuna flying boats.
No 1 (Operations) Squadron in British Columbia with Curtiss HS-2L flying boats.
No 2 (Operations) Squadron in Alberta with DH-4As, Avro 522As and 504Ns.
No 3 (Operations) Squadron at Rockcliffe, Ontario with Curtiss HS-2L, Vickers Viking, Vedette and Varuna flying boats.
No 4 (Operations) Squadron at Dartmouth, Nova Scotia with Curtiss HS-2L and Vickers Varuna flying boats.

Over the next few years the force was steadily expanded, though mainly with civil types, since 90 percent of flying continued to be devoted to civil operations, the balance to training. The Avro 504Ks had given way to 504Ns, while in 1927 the first of over 60 De Havilland DH 60 Moths was acquired, together with a number of Curtiss-Reid Ramblers. Some 36 Canadian-built Avro Avian Minor and Major trainers followed, plus some Vedette Mark VI amphibian versions of the now well-established flying boat and a single Ford 6-AT trimotor transport. In 1931 20 Fleet Fawn I trainers were added, together with some Avro 621 Tutors and Fairchild 71 sea-planes, the latter for survey and communications duties. By now the establishment had risen to a strength of 204 officers and 732 airmen, and although of very much lesser importance, the military side had not been entirely forgotten, a few Siskin III fighters and Atlas army co-operation aircraft having been acquired from Armstrong-Whitworth by 1930. However, the 1932 budget allocations indicated the government's priorities for the air force, with $15 million allocated for civil expenditure and $2.51 million for military use.

By now, however, the infamous Great Depression had arrived, and before 1932 was out, the first cuts were being made. Permanent Air Force establishment was savagely slashed to 103 officers and 591 airmen, but at the same time the civil involvement was considerably reduced, to be allowed in the future to be taken over mainly by the airlines and private sector. The Non-Permanent force was, in contrast, to be expanded and while the five existing regular units were disbanded, three new Auxiliary units were set up at Toronto, Vancouver and Winnipeg as 10, 11 and 12 Squadrons, together forming No. 1 Army Co-operation Wing; they were soon joined by 13 Squadron also. Although grandly named, the units were equipped almost entirely with small light aircraft such as the Moth.

In February 1933, 4 Squadron was re-formed at Vancouver as a new Permanent Force unit, equipped once again with flying boats. A little over a year later it was joined by a second such unit with the

Above: An Avro Avian trainer fitted with skis is seen here visiting Newfoundland seal fisheries.
Right: A Curtiss HS-2L flyingboat. These ex-Naval Air Service aircraft, the first water-borne aircraft to see service in Canada after World War I.

formation of 5 Squadron at Dartmouth, Nova Scotia. Before 1934 was out another Auxiliary unit had been formed when 15 Squadron came into being; this was to be the RCAF's first fighter unit, equipped with the Siskins.

Slowly the air force continued to regain its strength as political tension in Europe and Asia began to grow during the mid-thirties, and during 1935 a further two squadrons were to be formed. Both of these were re-formations, 2 Squadron returning to establishment in April and 3 Squadron in September. Both formed at Trenton, 2 Squadron then moving to Rockcliffe, Ontario; this latter unit was

Below: Curtiss-Reid Rambler trainers, acquired in 1927, seen on a snow-clad airfield at the time of delivery.

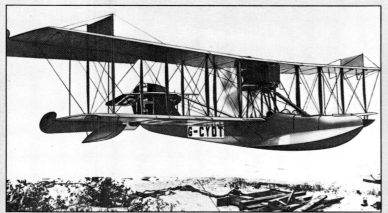

Above: The Fleet Fawn trainer was first acquired in 1931. One is seen here mounted on floats operating from a lakeside jetty.

Above: Fairchild 71 survey floatplane in flight.

formed for army co-operation work with the Atlas biplanes, while 3 Squadron was intended as a bomber unit. It was not to become so for many months in the event, for no suitable aircraft were available; eight Siskin IIIAs had been acquired to augment the earlier models of this aircraft, and with these a fighter flight was formed within 3 Squadron.

In 1936 there was to be much greater expansion, however, with three more Permanent Air Force units and four Auxiliaries forming. In January and February 7 and 8 Squadrons were born as General Purpose units, flying light aircraft from Ottawa and Winnipeg respectively. They were followed in March by 6 Squadron, formed as a torpedo-bomber unit with Vedettes at Trenton, where a Technical Testing Unit and Army Co-operation School were also now set up. During the summer, 18, 19, 20 and 21 Squadrons were all formed as Auxiliary bomber units – though without bombers. At Camp Borden also, expansion of training was taking place, a full training group being set up to include Air Armament, Flying Training, Navigation and Seaplane schools. 1 November saw the Department of Transport formed which at last freed the RCAF from nearly

Below: Eight Siskin IIIAs were purchased to augment the earlier Mark IIIs, these equipping a flight of 3 Squadron.

all its remaining civil responsibilities except photographic survey and a certain amount of air transport. Establishment of the Permanent Air Force was now increased to 249 officers and 1581 airmen, while the Non-Permanent Force went up to 163 officers and 861 men. Orders were placed in the United Kingdom for Westland Wapiti biplanes to equip the new bomber units, which began arriving during the following year. These went first to 3 Squadron, the Siskins then going to form a new 1 Squadron as a Permanent Force fighter unit.

A considerably expanded military aviation budget in 1937 – increased to an all-time high of $4.5 million – allowed substantial aircraft manufacture to begin. Seven of an eventual 18 Supermarine Stranraer flying boats were built under license to replace the elderly Vedettes, while the Ottawa Car manufacturing Co. began work on 18 Wapitis and Boeing of Vancouver produced 11 of 20 Blackburn Shark torpedo-bomber biplanes. The advent of more modern equipment was heralded by seven Canadian Vickers-built Northrop Delta monoplanes for the bomber squadrons, while Canadian Fairchild produced the prototype Bolingbroke I – a license-built version of the Bristol Blenheim IV bomber. Norduyn meanwhile had begun production in 1935 of the all-Canadian Norseman floatplane, and now obtained the rights to build the North American NA 16-3 Harvard. Other trainer types such as the DH Tiger Moth and Airspeed Oxford were also ordered.

The first Sharks went to re-equip the torpedo-bomber 6 Squadron, which moved to Vancouver, while as the Stranraers began to come off the line, 4 and 5 Squadrons were re-equipped. In 1937 5 Squadron ceased the work it had been doing for many months in support of the Royal Canadian Mounted Police, and became purely a Coastal Reconnaissance unit, while at the start of the following year 4 Squadron also ceased the last of the civil-orientated photographic work it had been involved on, and was redesignated a General Reconnaissance unit.

With the expansion plans then afoot it had become clear that the numbering of Permanent Force squadrons would soon impinge on those of the Auxiliaries, and consequently in November 1937 the latter all had the number 100 added to their titles to continue their differentiation. Thus 10, 12 and 13 Squadrons became 110, 112 and 113 Army Co-operation Squadrons; 11 Squadron became 111 Coastal Artillery Co-operation Squadron at Patricia Bay, British Columbia; 15 Fighter and 18, 19, 20 and 21 Bomber Squadrons became 115, 118, 119, 120 and 121 Squadrons respectively.

The year 1938 was marked by an enormous uplift in the budget to

Above: The RCAF's first fighter was the Armstrong-Whitworth Siskin III which equipped 15 Squadron initially; two of these biplanes are shown.
Right: One of the most numerous family of trainers with the RCAF during the interwar years, the de Havilland DH 60 Genet Moth.

$11.25 million – a figure which was to pale into insignificance following the Munich Crisis later in the year, when it was pushed up to $30 million. It was also a notable year for the RCAF, for on 19 November 1938 the force became independent, responsible directly to the Minister of National Defense. An Air Council was formed with Air Vice-Marshal G M Croil as the first Chief of Air Staff. Three further Auxiliary units were formed – 114 Bomber, 116 Coastal Artillery Co-operation and 117 Fighter Squadrons. At the same time the air force as a whole was reorganized in three Air Commands:

Left: One of the world's most famous trainers, the DH 82 Tiger Moth, was acquired in considerable numbers by the RCAF.
Above: The Armstrong-Whitworth Atlas army co-operation biplane served with 2 Squadron.
Right: Fleet Fawn II trainer.

Western Air Command: Headquarters in Vancouver, controlling five Regular and four Auxiliary squadrons.
Eastern Air Command: Headquarters in Halifax, controlling four Regular and four Auxiliary Squadrons and the Photo Establishment.
Air Training Command: Headquarters in Toronto, controlling one Regular and three Auxiliary squadrons, and the Training establishments.

During the year a British Air Mission arrived in Canada to seek the production of additional aircraft here for the Royal Air Force. Canadian Associated Aircraft Ltd was formed to build Handley-Page Hampden bombers, 80 of which were initially ordered, while the Canadian Car and Foundry Co (CCF) was given a license to construct the Hawker Hurricane I fighter and the Avro Anson crew trainer. The National Steel Car Corporation (NSC) of Toronto was to undertake production of the Westland Lysander, while Norduyn was to add the assembly of North American Yale trainers to production of Harvards and Norsemen.

Early in 1939 20 Hurricane Is were sent to Canada from Britain, including one pattern aircraft for CCF, the rest going to 1 Squadron in February. During the following August the first eight Fairey Battles arrived, while during that same month the first Lysanders rolled out of NSC's plant, going during the following month to equip 2 Squadron. Meanwhile 3 Squadron gave up its Wapitis and moved to Halifax to become a fighter squadron. In the event no new aircraft were to be received, and the unit was disbanded on 5 September, immediately after the outbreak of war in Europe.

Thus when Germany's invasion of Poland on 1 September 1939

Right: Acquired in 1936, the Westland Wapiti was the RCAF's first bomber aircraft, equipping some of the new auxiliary bomber squadrons.

threw Western Europe into a new war and the Canadian government mobilized its forces, the RCAF had grown considerably to reach a force of some 20 squadrons and a personnel strength of 4061 officers and men. That its equipment scarcely matched the new 'paper' strength of the air force was self-evident. There were 270 aircraft on hand:

Operational Types
22 Westland Wapitis
19 Hawker Hurricanes
13 AW Atlas
12 Vickers-Northrop Deltas
11 Blackburn Sharks
10 Fairey Battles
 8 Supermarine Stranraers
 5 AW Siskin IIIs
 4 Vickers Vancouvers

Training Types
41 Fleet Fawns
30 DH Tiger Moths
20 Airspeed Oxfords
14 NA Harvards
14 Avro Tutors & Prefects
 2 Hawker Tomtits

Transport Types
23 Fairchild 51s and 71s
 9 Vickers Vedettes
 8 Bellanca Pacemakers
 4 Norduyn Norsemen
 1 Grumman Goose

As in 1914, Canada was quick to come to the aid of the mother country across the other side of the Atlantic, and when the Dominion government declared war on Nazi Germany on 10 September, unit dispositions were as follows:

Eastern Air Command

10 (Bomber) Squadron	Wapiti
116 (Fighter) Squadron*	nil
5 (General Reconnaissance) Squadron	Stranraer
8 (General Purpose) Squadron	Delta
2 (Army Co-operation) Squadron	Atlas
117 (Coastal Artillery Co-op) Squadron*	nil
1 (Fighter) Squadron	Hurricane

Western Air Command

4 (General Reconnaissance) Squadron	Stranraer
6 (Torpedo-Bomber) Squadron	Shark
111 (Coastal Artillery Co-op) Squadron	Avro 621, 626
113 (Fighter) Squadron*	nil
120 (Bomber) Squadron	DH 82A

Air Training Command

110 (Army Co-operation) Squadron	Avro 626
114 (Bomber) Squadron	nil
119 (Bomber) Squadron	DH 82A

Air Force Headquarters

7 (General Purpose) Squadron	FC-71, Bellanca
115 (Fighter) Squadron	Fawn
118 (Bomber) Squadron	DH 60 Moth
121 (bomber) Squadron	nil

* Several Auxiliary units had been reallocated to the alternative duties shown during 1939.

Top: Modern trainers for the expanding RCAF – the North American Harvard was one of the types chosen for licence-production.
Far left: The Bellanca Pacemaker biplane was employed by 7 (General Purpose) Squadron for light transport and communications duties.
Near left: A Fairchild 71.
Below: A pair of Fairchild 51 floatplanes on a lake.

THE RCAF AT HOME
1939-45

The declaration of war preceded the main re-equipment of the RCAF, but as it soon became obvious that no major activity was likely to take place before the spring of 1940, further modernization and reorganization continued to take place through the rest of 1939. During this period there were several changes, 4 and 5 Flying Boat Squadrons both becoming restyled Bomber-Reconnaissance Squadrons tasked mainly with antisubmarine patrol on the west and east coasts respectively – a job in which they were joined by similarly restyled 6 and 8 Squadrons, and by newly formed 10 and 11 Squadrons with Wapitis – both the latter in Eastern Air Command. 119 and 120 Squadrons also became Bomber-Reconnaissance units on antisubmarine duties, while 118 Squadron became another Coastal Artillery Co-operation unit, initially using types like the Atlas, and subsequently Lysanders. During the fall 110 and 112 Squadrons started receiving Lysanders, but in December 2 Squadron was disbanded, its aircraft and personnel being used to raise these two units to full strength. Meanwhile 7, 113, 114, 116 and 117 Squadrons were also disbanded.

Canada was quick to send an air component to fight alongside the RAF in Europe, and early in 1940 three squadrons of the most modern types available were shipped over. 110 and 112 Squadrons, having been brought up to strength with Lysanders after the demise of 2 Squadron, made up the Army Co-operation element of this component, while 1 Squadron absorbed 115 Squadron to bring this unit fully up to establishment also, packing up its Hurricanes to provide the fighter element.

Meanwhile, however, the main initial function of the RCAF was to aid in the British Commonwealth Air Training Plan which was set up in December 1939. Designed to train aircrew from all over the Free World, the open spaces of Canada would provide a major element of the scheme, for which more than 4000 trainer aircraft were ordered. Instructors would be provided by the RAF, RCAF and the US, and initially the scheme was intended to run until 31 March 1943; in the event it was to be extended until 31 March 1945, by which time 131,553 aircrew would have been trained – 80 percent of them Canadian nationals. The size of the scheme grew steadily until 67 training schools – 21 of them double establishments – and ten specialist schools had been formed. Aircraft to be employed included 1500 Avro Ansons, 404 Tiger Moths with coupé hoods over the normally open cockpits, 400 Fleet Finches and 38 Norsemen. These were to be followed by 365 more Tiger Moths, nearly 800 Fairey Battles to operate as dual control and gunnery trainers and target tugs, 202 more Finches and 90 Fleet 60 Forts for advanced training. The US was to supply 282 Boeing-Stearman PT-27s, which would later be replaced by 1307 Fairchild M-62 Cornell Is (PT-26As) and 250 Mark IIs (PT-26Bs) to be built in Canada. Some 550 twin-engined Cessna T-50 Crane IAs were also to be supplied by the US. Many of the 225 Lysanders built in Canada were also to be employed in the training role, augmented by a further 102 from Britain. More Harvards, Yales and Norsemen were also to be supplied by Norduyn.

By October 1943 the scheme had grown to 97 flying schools and 184 ancillary units which had more than 10,000 training aircraft of all types in use. More than 3000 trainees were being poured out each

Below: Blackburn Sharks fitted with floats seen over Sea Island with 6 Squadron in 1938/39.

Previous pages: Over Canada's west coast patrolling Lockheed Hudson anti-submarine bombers return to base as the sun sets into the Pacific, watched by vigilant Bofors anti-aircraft gunners.

Above: The Fairey Battle light bomber was used widely in Canada as an advanced trainer.
Below: British Commonwealth Air Training Plan Fleet Finch IIs of 411 Elementary Flying Training School at Windsor Mills, Quebec. The aircraft are modified as were most open-cockpit trainers in Canada, with a 'glasshouse' coupe hood.

Above: Fleet Fort trainer at Calgary, Alberta.
Right: Designed and built in Canada – a Norduyn Norseman floatplane landing on a lake.

month by this time, and indeed by the early months of 1944 so great was the supply that it became possible to reduce output. The men trained during the war years would include 72,835 for the RCAF, 42,110 for the RAF (including 3333 for the Fleet Air Arm), 9606 for the Royal Australian Air Force and 7002 for the Royal New Zealand Air Force, demonstrating what a truly Dominion effort the scheme represented.

While this massive training effort was brought into being, the RCAF maintained two totally separate functions – and virtually two separate air forces. Firstly, there was the security and integrity of the homeland, which initially centered mainly around the war against the German U-Boats over the Western Atlantic and Canada's Eastern seaboard. As war with Japan approached, a similar function over the Pacific coast, coupled with a more active fighter defense and an involvement in Alaska alongside the USAAF, became necessary.

The second function was the building up and maintenance of an expeditionary air force to fight alongside the RAF on the various war fronts elsewhere in the world. In the execution of these functions the RCAF was to grow until it became the fourth largest of the Allied air forces involved in the war, outstripping not only the air forces of the other Dominions, but also of France and Co-belligerent Italy.

The Home Air Force

During the 'Phony War' period from September 1939 to May 1940, the remaining units of Eastern Air Command undertook anti-submarine patrols over the shipping leaving North American shores for Europe, and as the air component to serve in the war area was withdrawn, this command initially shrunk in size. Initially 8 Squadron with its Deltas and 5 Squadron's Stranraers were the most active, the former unit being increased in aircraft establishment as more Deltas came off the production line during early 1940. In November 1939 the first of 18 Bolingbroke Is had been accepted, and as production of these aircraft was stepped up, they were steadily delivered to 8 Squadron, the Deltas then moving to Western Air Command to replace the DH 82As in 120 Squadron. Two also went to 119 Squadron in Air Training Command. Production of Lysanders also allowed 111 Squadron to replace its little Avro trainers with these more potent aircraft, and in June 1940 this unit's designation was altered from Coastal Artillery to Army Co-operation, and then to Fighter – a duty little more appropriate for the

Right: Trainers at Camp Borden are reflected in melted snow waters; in the foreground is a North American Yale, while behind it is an Airspeed Oxford. To the right is a Northrop Nomad – an ex USAAC A-17A attack bomber, employed like the Fairey Battle as an advanced trainer.
Far right: Boeing-Stearman PT-27 trainer of the BCATP.

Lysander than had its previous role been for the Tutor! 118 Squadron was also redesignated a fighter unit, but lack of suitable aircraft led to the disbandment of this squadron in September 1940, and of 111 Squadron in the following February.

Production Hurricane Is had begun to appear off the CCF lines as early as January 1940, but due to the crisis which arose following the start of the German 'Blitzkrieg' in May, and to the prior call of the actual war front, most of the 40 built were shipped to England during the summer, followed by many of the 340 Mark Xs which followed. CCF had license-built the Grumman FF-1 two-seat biplane fighter for the Turkish government during 1937 (most aircraft actually finding their way to the Republicans in Spain during the Civil War). To keep the lines working until Hurricane production could be instituted, the government was persuaded to accept a batch of 15 of these aircraft, to be known as GE 23 Goblins. Not filling any duty adequately, they were not wanted by the RCAF, but given them during 1940, 118 Squadron was re-formed at Rockcliffe in December – initially on a one flight basis – and subsequently moved to Dartmouth, Nova Scotia, where the aircraft were used for coastal patrol and reconnaissance.

This marked the first formation of a new operational unit in Canada since the outbreak of war, although earlier in the year 12 Squadron had been formed with various light aircraft as a Communications unit, together with 13 Squadron which was set up

Above: Airspeed Oxford crew trainers at Rockliffe, Ontario in 1942.
Below: Liberator VI transport in flight from Rockliffe in 1945.

at Vancouver as an operational training unit for seaplane and bomber-reconnaissance crews.

Other aircraft were needed urgently, and 151 Mark IV versions of the Bolingbroke were ordered, the first of which had appeared before the end of 1940. 14 amphibian versions of the Consolidated Catalina flying boat, known to the RAF as Catalina IAs, but dubbed Canso in RCAF service, were purchased direct from the USA, while arrangements were made for both the PBY-5 flying boat and the -5A amphibian to be built by Boeing of Canada and Canadian Vickers. As a stop-gap 20 Douglas DB-280 bombers – the USAAF's B-18A – were acquired as the Digby, issue of these aircraft being made to 10 Squadron to replace the aging Wapitis as quickly as possible.

Throughout 1941, as the crisis situation in Europe subsided, efforts in Canada were concentrated mainly on the development of the Air Training Plan, and on production of aircraft to be employed in the United Kingdom, and in the new Middle East theater. Gradually, however, new units could be formed as personnel and aircraft not required for immediate overseas service became available. During June 116 Squadron was re-formed with the new Catalinas and Cansos to provide Eastern Air Command with some more modern and long-ranging flying boat equipment, while others of these aircraft would subsequently go to 5 Squadron.

Growing tension between Japan and the US resulted in the need to strengthen and upgrade Western Air Command, and here in August two new units were formed. 115 Squadron was equipped with Bolingbrokes fitted with under-fuselage gun packs, operating in a fighter guise, while 117 Squadron was to join 4 Squadron in the bomber-reconnaissance role with Stranraers. As the Bolingbroke IVs started to flow from Fairchild's factory, they went not only to 8 Squadron in the East, but to bring 119 Squadron up to strength. 123 Squadron was formed meanwhile as an Army Co-operation training unit with Lysanders and Harvards.

It had by now become clear that war with Japan could not be long delayed. Canada still had virtually no fighter defense, since all available Hurricanes had gone to Europe. Orders for Bell P-39 Airacobras had not been fulfilled, yet but urgent pleas were made to the RAF, which eventually, and with some reluctance, released 72 Curtiss Kittyhawk IA fighters from among the AK and AL serial blocks. Deliveries direct from the US began during October 1941 and quantities of Lockheed Hudson IIIAs were also released. The arrival of the Kittyhawks allowed 111 Squadron to be re-formed with these aircraft at Rockcliffe at the start of November, while later in the month 118 Squadron converted to these aircraft from the

Above: CCF-built Grumman FF-1 Goblins of 118 Squadron in formation in 1941. These are operated from Rockliffe, and then Dartmouth, Nova Scotia, in the coastal patrol role.

Goblins, which were then passed to 123 Squadron for training duties. At this time, however, the recently re-formed 117 Squadron was again disbanded. It was replaced in the West by two new units which were formed on 8/9 December, just as the Japanese attacks on Allied bases in the Pacific and southeast Asia began. 7 Squadron received Sharks initially, while 9 Squadron formed with Stranraers.

The outbreak of hostilities with Japan brought a new dimension to the war, placing western Canada close to the fighting zone. At once the newly formed 111 Squadron was ordered to Patricia Bay, Vancouver Island, while 8 Squadron moved from Nova Scotia to Sea Island, Vancouver. Only the latter was immediately ready, however, 111 Squadron under its Battle of Britain veteran commander, Sqn Ldr A Deane Nesbitt, not being declared fully operational until mid-March 1942, by which time it had crashed several of its Kittyhawks, one pilot losing his life.

Now the home-based RCAF really began to expand, a further Kittyhawk fighter squadron forming in January, together with a ferry unit (124 Squadron) and two Composite Squadrons (121 and 122); the former was to undertake target towing and other such duties, and would include in its strength such exotic types as Boeing 247D transports, while 122 amalgamated the various coastal

Above: Wg Cdr G R McGregor DFC, ex-Battle of Britain pilot, commanded X Wing in Alaska in 1942.
Right: Sqn Ldr A Deane Nesbitt DFC commanded the first RCAF Kittyhawk unit, 111 Squadron, early in 1942. He had previously flown Hurricanes with 1 Squadron in England in summer 1940.
Below: Liberator V of 10(BR) Squadron prepares to take off from an east coast base in summer 1943.

Artillery Co-operation elements in the West, flying Norsemen, Sharks, Lysanders and Goose amphibians. In February 113 Squadron re-formed in the East as a bomber-reconnaissance unit with some of the Hudsons, but the biggest expansion occurred between April and July. With the crisis in the West, quantities of Hurricane XIs and XIIs were retained from production, and in this period eight new fighter squadrons came into being. These were:

West Coast

132 Squadron	Kittyhawks
133 Squadron	Kittyhawks and Hurricanes
135 Squadron	Kittyhawks and Hurricanes

East Coast

125 Squadron	Hurricanes
126 Squadron	Hurricanes
130 Squadron	Kittyhawks and Hurricanes
128 Squadron	Hurricanes
127 Squadron	Hurricanes

In this same period 117 squadron was again re-formed, this time with Cansos in the East, together with the similarly equipped 162 Squadron and 145 Squadron on Hudsons. In the West 147 Squadron was formed with Bolingbrokes.

As soon as the United States had been brought into the war, close liaison with US forces had been established, and during April the Bolingbroke fighters of 115 Squadron were moved up to US territory, being based on Annette Island to aid in the air defense of Alaska. At the end of May General DeWitt, US Army commander on the Pacific coast, requested the deployment of a further RCAF fighter squadron and a bomber-reconnaissance unit to Yakutat, Alaska, to support the limited USAAF units available. Consequently 8 and 111 Squadrons moved up, forming X Wing for the defense of south Alaska, while the remaining US air strength shifted into the north and west area, and the Aleutians, where Japanese landings at Kiska and Attu Islands took place on 6 June 1942. With the departure of these units, 118 and 132 Squadrons moved their Kittyhawks to British Columbia. 132 took up station at Patricia Bay while 118 joined 115 Squadron on Annette Island, where the two units formed Y Wing for the defense of British Columbia and the Alaskan 'panhandle'. The arrival of the Kittyhawks relieved 115 Squadron of the fighter duties in which their Bolingbrokes would have been quite inadequate against Japan's carrier planes; with gun packs removed, the unit returned to a bomber-reconnaissance role.

During June 8 and 111 Squadrons arrived in Alaska, 111 Squadron taking up base at Elmendorf from where it could provide cover for the Anchorage area. No long-range tanks were available at first, and all areas where the Japanese were to be found were beyond the range of the unit's aircraft. Wing commander was Wg Cdr G R McGregor, who had flown with 1 Squadron during its Battle of Britain debut in England, and then commanded 2 Squadron, and who had been credited with four victories against German aircraft before his return to Canada. McGregor felt strongly that RCAF units should not be employed in action by the US commanders if any USAAF units were available, even if the latter were less-experienced. Representations were made that the Canadians should play a more active role, and in July 111 Squadron was ordered to move up to Umnak, the advanced US base in the Aleutians. The weather in Alaska was dreadful, with much cloud and sudden fogs which could ground units for days. 111 had already lost one aircraft due to a fire following technical trouble, when on 16 July seven Kittyhawks and three US C-47 transports took off for the last leg of the flight, from Cold Bay to Umnak. A sudden fog developed with disastrous consequences; one fighter pilot became lost and wandered out over the sea, not being seen again, while four more and one of the transports flew into a mountainside. In three days the squadron had lost seven aircraft and five pilots, including their new commanding officer, Sqn Ldr Kerwin.

Meanwhile the first major success for Western Air Command units had occurred on 7 July. On this date F/Sgt P M G Thomas of 115 Squadron while on an antisubmarine patrol in his Bolingbroke, saw and attacked the Japanese submarine Ro 32. Sufficiently severe damage was inflicted to immobilize the vessel, and Thomas directed US destroyers to the area, these administering the 'coup de grace'.

At Umnak the depleted 111 Squadron discovered that the USAAF had plenty of P-40E aircraft but were short of pilots. Ten Canadians were therefore attached to the US 11th Fighter Squadron as F Flight until late August, when nine new P-40Ks were provided for the squadron by the Americans. During September 1942 a new base at Adak was completed, from which raids by fighters could be made on the Japanese base at Kiska, from where the enemy was operating Nakajima A6M2-N 'Rufe' floatplane fighters. The new commanding officer of 111 Squadron, Sqn Ldr K A Boomer, requested that RCAF representation be included in one of the early raids here, and on 26 September he led four Canadian-manned

Below: A few Spitfire Vs were sent to Canada and were employed, like this one at Rockliffe, for photographic duties.

P-40Ks to undertake flak suppression duties during such an attack. He was able to engage and shoot down an intercepting 'Rufe' – the only aerial victory of the war for the home-based RCAF. Shortly after this success, however, the squadron was ordered back to Anchorage, moving then to Umnak again to provide defense for the US naval base at Kodiak Island.

In Canada meantime, one further Hurricane fighter squadron had been formed on the east coast (129). Toward the end of October a new type came into service when 149 Squadron was formed in Western Air Command with Bristol Beaufort torpedo-bombers, but a few days later the Vancouver-based 13 Squadron, operating as an operational training unit for flying boat crews, was disbanded. This period, however, saw the first concrete success for Eastern Air Command when on 30 October 1942 Flt Lt D F Raynes, flying a 10 Squadron Digby, serial 747, and carrying the codes JK—K, sank a German U-Boat (U.520) – the culmination of several attacks made by this unit during the year.

Some 10,000 aircraft were ordered in Canada in 1942, including such advanced types as the Lancaster X and Mosquito. By the end of the year deliveries of new types – particularly those built by the country's own industry – ensured that the Order of Battle on 1 January 1943 was very different from that three years earlier:

Eastern Air Command HQ Halifax, Nova Scotia

10 (BR) Squadron	Digby
11 (BR) Squadron	Hudson III
116 (BR) Squadron	Catalina
117 (BR) Squadron	Canso
126 (F) Squadron	Hurricane I
129 (F) Squadron	Hurricane I
121 (Comp) Squadron	various
113 (BR) Squadron	Hudson III
162 (BR) Squadron	Canso A
119 (BR) Squadron	Hudson III
128 (F) Squadron	Hurricane I
130(F) Squadron	Hurricane XII

1 Group; HQ St Johns, Newfoundland

5 (BR) Squadron	Canso A
127 (F) Squadron	Hurricane I
145 (BR) Squadron	Hudson III
125 (F) Squadron	Hurricane I

12 Operational Training Group

31 (RAF) OTU	ferry
32 (RAF) OTU	torpedo-bomber
34 (RAF) OTU	long-range bomber
1 (RCAF) OTU	fighter
3 (RCAF) OTU	bomber-reconnaissance

Western Air Command

2 Group; HQ Victoria, British Columbia

4 (BR) Squadron	Canso A
14 (F) Squadron	Kittyhawk IA
120 (BR) Squadron	Stranraer
122 (Comp) Squadron	various
132 (F) Squadron	Kittyhawk IA
133 (F) Squadron	Hurricane XII
135 (F) Squadron	Hurricane XII
147 (BR) Squadron	Bolingbroke IV
149 (TB) Squadron	Beaufort

4 Group; HQ Prince Rupert, British Columbia

6 (BR) Squadron	Stranraer
7 (BR) Squadron	Shark
9 (BR) Squadron	Stranraer

RCAF Detached Operations – Alaska
X Wing, Anchorage

8 (BR) Squadron	Bolingbroke IV
111 (F) Squadron	Kittyhawk IA and P-40K

Y Wing, Annette Island

115 (BR) Squadron	Bolingbroke IV
118 (F) Squadron	Kittyhawk IA

Air Force Headquarters, Ottawa

12 (Comm) Squadron	various
124 (Ferry) Squadron	various

British Commonwealth Air Training Plan
No 1 Training Command
No 2 Training Command
No 3 Training Command
No 4 Training Command

In Alaska the winter of 1942/43 saw little flying as the local weather really clamped down. As spring returned, however, the Kittyhawk pilots of 111 Squadron began training for fighter-bomber operations – training which was to stand them in good stead. X Wing changed its composition in March 1943 when 14 Squadron arrived to replace 8 Squadron. During the following month this unit moved up to Amchitka where 24 P-40Ks were available as a pool, pilots operating on a three days on/one day off basis, maintaining three flights each of eight US pilots and one of Canadians. On 18 April the American offensive to retake Kiska began, and during the next month the 14 Squadron pilots were to engage in 14 missions totalling 88 sorties, strafing and bombing targets in the area. In mid-May the unit was replaced by 111 Squadron's pilots, who flew a similar tour. Each unit flew a further tour, and then in July 111 Squadron handed its remaining Kittyhawk IAs at Umnak to 14 Squadron and returned to Canada. Following a final round of operations during August, 14 Squadron also returned in September, the Aleutians campaign being virtually at an end.

In Canada further new aircraft were put into service during 1943, and several more units were formed. Local production of Catalinas and Cansos was much increased during the year, while major types

Left: The RCAF's most numerous flyingboat type during the early war years was the licence-built Supermarine Stranraer. An aircraft of 5 Squadron is seen here in flight over a four-masted schooner.
Above right: Bristol Beaufort torpedo-bomber of 149 Squadron.
Below: The only aerial victory to be claimed by a member of the RCAF over the Aleutians was credited to Sqn Ldr K A Boomer of 111 Squadron on 26 September 1942.

acquired from the US included Lockheed Ventura GRVs and Consolidated Liberator IIIs and Vs for the bomber-reconnaissance squadrons, and Lockheed Lodestars and Douglas Dakotas for transport duties. Production of Hurricanes had ended with a total built of 1077, many of the later models having been despatched to Russia. The Bolingbroke IV – many of which had been built with Pratt & Whitney Twin Wasp Junior or Wright Cyclone engines in place of the Bristol Mercury – had completed production as a bomber after the 151st of this version, but had been ordered back into production as a trainer in which role some hundreds saw service with the BCAT Plan. A single aircraft had been completed with Edo floats during 1942 as the Mark III, and this aircraft saw service with 5 Squadron. Other deliveries by the end of 1943 included 55 Cansos, 193 Catalinas and 216 Hudson IIIs, Vs and VIs.

New units formed included 13 Squadron, formed again as a photographic unit with Hurricanes and a few Spitfires delivered from the United Kingdom; this unit would later receive some B-25 Mitchells, delivered from the US. In the same month, January 1943, the RCAF's first specialist transport unit, 164 Squadron, was formed, equipped with Lodestars and Dakotas, and this was followed in July by the similarly equipped 165 Squadron. 168 Squadron was to be formed in October as a heavy transport unit with a mixture of converted Liberators and Boeing B-17 Fortresses, augmented by further Lodestars and Dakotas.

10 Squadron received Libertors during the spring, the Digbys going to form a new 161 Squadron, which subsequently added Canso amphibians to its strength. On 3 May 160 Squadron was the last new operational unit to form, operating Cansos on the west coast. Its formation was, however, followed by that of two new communications units, 167 on the east coast and 166 on the west, which came into existence in August and September respectively with a variety of light types. 163 Squadron had been formed in March as an army co-operation unit with Bolingbrokes. Operating within Western Air Command, it received a number of Hurricanes during June, while the sole torpedo-bomber squadron, 149, was redesignated a bomber-reconnaissance unit at this time and, along with 113, 115 and 145 Squadrons, re-equipped with Venturas.

As the fall of 1943 approached, 10 Squadron's new Liberators enjoyed an upsurge of success against the U-Boats, which were now losing the Battle of the Atlantic. On 19 September Flt Lt R F Fisher destroyed U.341 flying Liberator 586, JK-A, while little more than a month later on 26 October Flt Lt R M Aldwinkle sank U.420. A 5 Squadron Canso also sank a further U-Boat, and by the war's end Eastern Air Command would have destroyed six U-Boats.

As is so often the case when an air force has reached its optimum strength, no sooner had this point been reached than the home-based RCAF began to shrink – and to shrink rapidly. By now the threat in the Pacific was much-reduced as the US forces now had the Japanese almost wholly on the defensive. In Europe an invasion of France was now in prospect and a Canadian army was to take part. Further build-up of the RCAF in the UK was required, and now units from the home air force could be spared as reinforcements for the first time since early 1940. Consequently during the final quarter of 1943 six fighter squadrons were selected for service overseas, all departing late in the year to form two new wings, one of fighters, the other of fighter-bombers. The units involved were:

14 Squadron (Kittyhawks)– became 442 Squadron
111 Squadron (Kittyhawks)– became 440 Squadron
118 Squadron (Kittyhawks)– became 438 Squadron
123 Squadron (Hurricanes) – became 439 Squadron
125 Squadron (Hurricanes) – became 441 Squadron
127 Squadron (Hurricanes) – became 443 Squadron

On their return from Alaska, the Kittyhawk squadrons had been re-equipped with new P-40N Kittyhawk IVs, 35 of which had been supplied to the RCAF during the year, but these were now passed to 163 Squadron, which changed its role from army co-operation to fighter, taking the place of the three older Kittyhawk units in the West.

By the end of the year U-Boat activity in the Western Atlantic was greatly reduced and controlled, and during December 117 Squadron was disbanded for the third time, while in January 1944 162 Squadron was loaned to RAF Coastal Command, flying across the Atlantic to operate from Wick in the northeast of Scotland.

The RCAF's overseas effort was now at a very high level – particularly in RAF Bomber Command – and the opportunity to reduce the level of operational strength at home was a welcome one. During March 1944 six more units were written off the Order of Battle – this time by disbandment. Three units from each command were affected:

Eastern Air Command
119 (BR) Squadron	Hudson
128 (F) Squadron	Hurricane
130 (F) Squadron	Hurricane

Western Air Command
147 (BR) Squadron	Bolingbroke
149 (BR) Squadron	Ventura
163 (F) Squadron	Kittyhawk IV

The final new formations in Canada during the war included 170 Ferry Squadron formed in March and a re-formed 14 Squadron as a photographic unit with Ansons and Dakotas during the summer. In June a new Northwestern Air Command was set up with Headquarters in Edmonton to administer the chain of airfields up to Alaska which were now mainly used by the transport units. Contraction remained the order of the day, however, and by the end of October a further six squadrons had gone:

Eastern Air Command
113 (BR) Squadron	Ventura
129 (F) Squadron	Hurricane

Western Air Command
9 (BR) Squadron	Canso
115 (BR) Squadron	Ventura
120 (BR) Squadron	Canso, Catalina
132 (F) Squadron	Kittyhawk IA

During early 1945 one of the two remaining fighter squadrons in the west, 133, added some Mosquitos to its strength, but the end of the wars to east and west was to complete the cycle of disbandments to an almost total degree. No further units were stood down until after the fall of Germany in early May, but thereafter the rundown was fast, and by the time of the Japanese surrender a dozen more had gone:

Eastern Air Command
5 (BR) Squadron	Canso
8 (BR) Squadron	Bolingbroke
10 (BR) Squadron	Liberator
116 (BR) Squadron	Canso, Catalina
126 (F) Squadron	Hurricane
145 (BR) Squadron	Ventura
161 (BR) Squadron	Canso
162 (BR) Squadron	Canso

Western Air Command
4 (BR) Squadron	Canso, Catalina
6 (BR) Squadron	Canso
7 (BR) Squadron	Canso, Catalina
160 (BR) Squadron	Canso

Above: Lockheed Lodestar transports of 165 (T) Squadron.
Below: Water-borne aircraft types of Western Air Command. In the foreground is a Fairchild 71, behind which can be seen a Vancouver II, a Stranraer and a Shark.

Following the end of the Pacific War nine of the remaining few units had disappeared by November, and these were:

Eastern Air Command

| 11 (BR) Squadron | Liberator |
| 167 (Comm) Squadron | various |

Western Air Command

122 (Comp) Squadron	various
133 (F) Squadron	Hurricane, Kittyhawk, Mosquito
135 (F) Squadron	Hurricane, Kittyhawk
165 (T) Squadron	Lodestar, Dakota
166 (Comm) Squadron	various

121 (Comp) and 170 (Ferry) Squadrons were also disbanded during this period, while in April 1946, the Heavy Transport 168 Squadron also met its end. The RCAF at home was down to just five squadrons – and not one of them equipped with operational types!

Squadron Code Letters Carried by Home-Based RCAF Aircraft, 1939-45

(NB codes were changed in many cases during 1942, and squadron allocations are indicated as pre or post this date)

AE	130 Squadron		MK	13 Squadron pre 42
AP	13 Squadron post 42		MX	120 Squadron pre 42
AQ	14 Squadron		OP	3 Squadron
	Photo unit, 44-45		OY	11 Squadron pre 42
BA	125 Squadron		PB	10 Squadron pre 42
BF	14 Squadron pre 42		PQ	117 Squadron post 42
BK	115 Squadron pre 42		QE	12 Squadron
BO	4 Squadron post 42		QN	5 Squadron pre 42
BV	126 Squadron		RA	128 Squadron
DE	5 Squadron post 42		RE	118 Squadron pre 42
DM	119 Squadron pre 42		RS	120 Squadron post 42
EA	145 Squadron		SZ	147 Squadron
EX	117 Squadron pre 42		TF	127 Squadron
FG	7 Squadron		TM	111 Squadron pre 42
FN	133 Squadron		UV	115 Squadron post 42
FY	4 Squadron pre 42		VD	123 Squadron
GR	119 Squadron post 42		VW	118 Squadron post 42
HA	129 Squadron		XE	6 Squadron
HJ	9 Squadron post 42		XP	135 Squadron
JK	10 Squadron post 42		YA	14 Squadron
KA	9 Squadron pre 42			post 42/pre 44
KL	11 Squadron post 42		YO	8 Squadron
KO	2 Squadron		ZM	149 Squadron
LZ	111 Squadron post 42		ZR	132 Squadron

Main Aircraft Types in Service with the RCAF in Canada, 1940-45, and the Units in which they Served

Supermarine Stranraer
4 (BR) Squadron
5 (BR) Squadron
6 (BR) Squadron
9 (BR) Squadron
117 (BR) Squadron
120 (BR) Squadron

Fairchild-Bristol Bolingbroke
8 (BR) Squadron
115 (F & BR) Squadron
119 (BR) Squadron
121 (Comp) Squadron
122 (Comp) Squadron
147 (BR) Squadron
163 (AC) Squadron

Hawker Hurricane
1 (F) Squadron
123 (F) Squadron
125 (F) Squadron
126 (F) Squadron
127 (F) Squadron
128 (F) Squadron
129 (F) Squadron
130 (F) Squadron
133 (F) Squadron
135 (F) Squadron
163 (AC) Squadron

Consolidated Liberator
10 (BR) Squadron
11 (BR) Squadron
168 (HT) Squadron

Lockheed Lodestar
164 (T) Squadron
165 (T) Squadron
168 (HT) Squadron

Vickers-Northrop Delta
8 (BR) Squadron
119 (BR) Squadron
120 (BR) Squadron

Westland Lysander
2 (AC) Squadron
110 (AC) Squadron
111 (CAC) Squadron
112 (AC) Squadron
118 (CAC) Squadron
122 (Comp) Squadron
123 (AC) Squadron

Bristol Beaufort
149 (TB) Squadron

Curtiss Kittyhawk
14 (F) Squadron
111 (F) Squadron
118 (F) Squadron
130 (F) Squadron
132 (F) Squadron
133 (F) Squadron
135 (F) Squadron
163 (F) Squadron

Consolidated Catalina
4 (BR) Squadron
6 (BR) Squadron
7 (BR) Squadron
9 (BR) Squadron
116 (BR) Squadron
117 (BR) Squadron
120 (BR) Squadron

Douglas Dakota
164 (T) Squadron
165 (T) Squadron
168 (HT) Squadron

Blackburn Shark
4 (BR) Squadron
6 (BR) Squadron
7 (BR) Squadron

CCF-Grumman GE-23 Goblin
118 (F) Squadron
123 (Tr) Squadron

Douglas Digby
10 (BR) Squadron
161 (BR) Squadron

Lockheed Hudson
11 (BR) Squadron
113 (BR) Squadron
119 (BR) Squadron
120 (BR) Squadron
145 (BR) Squadron

Lockheed Ventura
113 (BR) Squadron
115 (BR) Squadron
145 (BR) Squadron
149 (BR) Squadron

Consolidated Canso
4 (BR) Squadron
5 (BR) Squadron
6 (BR) Squadron
7 (BR) Squadron
9 (BR) Squadron
116 (BR) Squadron
117 (BR) Squadron
120 (BR) Squadron
160 (BR) Squadron
161 (BR) Squadron
162 (BR) Squadron

Left: Kittyhawk IAs of 111 Squadron over Alaska during 1942.

THE RCAF OVERSEAS
1940-46

The first RCAF unit to reach the United Kingdom was 110 Squadron, which arrived at Odiham late in February 1940 with its Lysander IIs. Before it could become operational the fighting in France had come to a close with the withdrawal of the British Expeditionary Force, and the capitulation of the French. As a result it was to be many months before the unit had an opportunity to fly operationally. Its arrival was followed in June by that of 1 Squadron, which was to be based at Middle Wallop airfield. Their Hurricanes required modification to bring them up to latest RAF standards, and August was halfway through before they were ready for action. By then the Battle of Britain was well underway, and it was into the face of the Luftwaffe's great assault on Fighter Command's southern airfields that the Canadians were first thrown.

The unit was to operate initially under the wing of the experienced 111 Squadron, RAF. Several pilots had been attached to this unit at its Northolt base early in August to gain operational experience, and Sqn Ldr E A McNab gained the RCAF's first victory when he claimed a Do17 shot down on 15th of that month. A few days later 1 Squadron was declared operational and moved from its recent training base at Croydon to Northolt. From this west London airfield in AVM Keith Park's No 11 group, it first entered action on 26 August.

This initial experience of operations proved expensive as the enthusiastic Canadians pressed home their attack on a formation of Do17s. While two of the bombers were claimed shot down by McNab and one of the flight commanders, Flt Lt G R McGregor, return fire from the rear gunners proved more effective than had been allowed for, and three Hurricanes were critically hit. While McNab and another pilot managed to crash-land, Flg Off R L Edwards became the unit's (and the RCAF's) first pilot to be killed in action.

The days that followed were to bring mixed fortunes for the Canadians – as for many other Hurricane squadrons – as they continued to take a toll of the raiders, but at a considerable cost (in aircraft, if not in pilots) to the escorting German fighters. During the next three weeks 14 victories were claimed, but 12 Hurricanes were shot down, although only one more pilot lost his life. Thereafter the unit seemed to have found its feet, for although several more engagements were to be fought during late September and early October, no further losses were to be sustained. The best day proved to be 27 September when seven Luftwaffe aircraft were claimed shot down. Three Bf 109Es were added on 5 October, and by the 11th, when the unit moved away north for a rest, 29 victories had been claimed for the loss of 15 Hurricanes, with two pilots dead and seven wounded. Decorations soon followed for the more successful pilots, DFCs going to Sqn Ldr McNab, Flt Lt McGregor, Flg Off A D Nesbitt and Plt Off B D Russel. McNab had already departed for Canada to pass on his experience to new pilots, his place being taken by Sqn Ldr E M Reyno.

Before leaving the Battle of Britain period, mention must be made of 242 Squadron – the RAF's 'All-Canadian' unit. Formed in October 1939 from Canadian personnel serving in the RAF, the unit was even commanded by an officer seconded from the RCAF – Sqn Ldr F M Gobeil – and at one time was intended for transfer to the RCAF, although in the event this was never to occur. When the German offensive broke out in Western Europe on 10 May 1940 the newly operational squadron was rushed to Church Fenton with its Hurricanes, and was at once in action, detaching flights to operate from airfields in France. In the first ten days of action some six victories were gained in the difficult circumstances of the initial Allied retreat, for the loss of four pilots, one of whom was killed. Moved to Biggin Hill, the squadron then operated over Dunkirk

Previous pages: Curtiss Tomahawk Is of 400 Squadron, Army Co-operation Command, on a training sorties from Odimah, Hants. They are AH806 'W' and AH785 'S' respectively.

Above: Wg Cdr B D Russel DSO, DFC★ who served with 1 Squadron during the Battle of Britain during 1940 and rose to become a successful Wing Leader.
Above right: First pilot of 1 Squadron, RCAF, to claim a German aircraft shot down over England was the commanding officer, Sqn Ldr E A McNab DFC, seen here in the cockpit of his Hurricane.
Below: Pilots sprint to a pair of 402 Squadron Hurricanes for a convoy patrol off the coast of north-east England in 1941.

during late May and early June. Here a substantial additional number of victories was claimed, but casualties had risen to 15 by the end of May.

Partially brought up to strength with new pilots, not all of whom were Canadians, the unit was then posted to France to support the remaining British forces there, who were retreating south of the River Seine. This was probably 242's most difficult period, and though losses were light in the air, and more successes were claimed, nearly all equipment and many of the ground party were left behind in France when the squadron again withdrew on 18 June. The unit's most successful pilot during this period was Plt Off W L 'Willie' McKnight, who was awarded a DFC. Re-established at Coltishall, the unit was taken over by a famous British fighter pilot, the legless Dougls Bader, and received an influx of new pilots – again many not being Canadians.

During the Battle of Britain the unit played a notable and well-recorded part, but with the arrival of 1 Squadron, RCAF, there was now no longer any intention to transfer the unit, and as the year wore on its all-Canadian identity was steadily diluted with a growing stream of British and Free-European arrivals. McKnight had raised

his personal score to 16½ by the end of the Battle, and added a Bar to his DFC before his death during an early offensive sortie over France on 12 January 1941. Other successful Canadians pilots decorated while with the unit included Flt Lt P S 'Stan' Turner, Flt Lt Roberts Grassick and Plt Offs Noel Stansfeld and John Latta. Another Canadian with the RAF who had achieved great success during this period was Sqn Ldr M H 'Hilly' Brown, who flew in France and Britain with the RAF's 1 Squadron, which he had commanded since November 1940. Credited with 14 and several shared victories, he was later to be killed in action as a Wing Commander, while flying from Malta in 1941. Among other RAF Canadians, Sqn Ldr John Kent had claimed seven of his final score of 13 by the end of 1940, and was leading the famous 92 Squadron, after commanding the all-Polish 303 Squadron; 249 Squadron was about to come under the command of Sqn Ldr R A 'Butch' Barton, who had gained six and four shared victories with the unit during 1940, and would add five more over Malta during the following year.

Meanwhile the second army co-operation unit, 112 Squadron, had arrived in the United Kingdom without aircraft late in 1940, and in December the personnel, with a number of volunteers from 110

Squadron, were formed into a second Canadian fighter unit as 2 Squadron, RCAF, at Digby. Hurricane Is were supplied, and in January 1941 G R McGregor was posted in from 1 Squadron as commanding officer, the squadron being declared operational at the end of February.

With the emergency of 1940 over, thought could now be given to organizational matters, and at the start of March 1941 the three RCAF units in the UK were renumbered to prevent confusion with 1, 2 and 110 Squadrons, RAF. 110 Squadron then became 400 Squadron, while 1 and 2 Squadrons became 401 and 402 respectively. All other RCAF units to be formed for service in Europe would receive numbers in this sequence, the range 400-449 being retained for the RCAF. At the same time a fourth unit was formed at Baginton as 403 Squadron, for the army co-operation role, and at once began equipping with US-built Curtiss Tomahawk fighters, which it had been decided would supplement the slow and ill-defined Lysanders in this role. 400 Squadron also began receiving these new aircraft in the following month, but in May 403's role was changed to that of fighter, and it moved to Ternhill, the Tomahawks being replaced by Spitfire Is.

The RCAF was now beginning to expand fast as the first products of the great aircrew training scheme began to flow across the Atlantic. April 1941 saw formation of the first bomber unit when 405 Squadron was set up at Driffield in North Yorkshire with Wellington II aircraft, while during May 404 and 407 Squadrons were both formed at Thorney Island to serve with Coastal Command; initially they were respectively equipped with Blenheim IVF long-range fighters and Blenheim IV bombers; the latter were replaced in June by Lockheed Hudsons. In Fighter Command 406 Squadron formed during the same month as a night fighter unit with Beaufighter IIs, while during June 409 and 410 Squadrons also formed as night fighters – initially with Boulton Paul Defiants – while 411 and 412 Squadrons formed as day fighter units at Digby with Spitfires. 408 Squadron also formed in June with Hampdens as the second RCAF bomber unit.

In July 413 Squadron formed at Stranraer in Scotland as a Catalina flying boat unit, while on 1 August 415 Squadron also formed in Coastal Command at Thorney Island as a torpedo-bomber unit with Beauforts and Blenheim IVs. When 414 Squadron came into being at Croydon that month as another army co-operation unit with Lysanders and Tomahawks, the RCAF in Britain had increased from three squadrons to 17 in less than eight months! These included five day and three night units in Fighter Command; two units with Bomber Command; four units with Coastal Command; and two with Army Co-operation Command.

Left: Handley-Page Halifax II of 405 Squadron, soon to become the mid-war stalwart of the RCAF bomber units.
Below: A Hurricane I of 401 Squadron, carrying the unit's YO code letters, is jacked-up for gun harmonization at Prestwick during 1940.

Fighter Command – the Day Fighters, 1941-43

The Canadian fighters resumed operations when 402 Squadron flew a sweep over France on 15 April 1941 with the Wittering Wing. Few squadrons were still flying Hurricane Is on front-line duties by this time, and in May the now-outdated fighters were replaced by Mark IIAs, followed by 12-gun IIBs in August. With these latter aircraft a full round of sweeps and escorts over the English Channel began forthwith. 401 Squadron, also equipped with these aircraft since February, had resumed operations from Digby on 23 July, and was active throughout August, joined in that month by 403 Squadron. With training complete, the latter unit had moved first to Hornchurch and then to Debden, exchanging its initial Spitfire IIAs for the latest Mark VBs at the same time.

Thus started a long period of cross-Channel operations which for the first year and a half were to bring little joy or notable success to the Canadian units. Operating against the veterans of the Luftwaffe fighter force still based in France and the Low Countries, with a sea crossing before and after any engagement, the RCAF units found themselves in a similar position to other RAF squadrons. Units were now composed to a large extent of new pilots, fresh from the Commonwealth Air Training Scheme, with only a leavening of experienced personnel to lead and guide. Fighters flew in Wing strength, often two, three or four Wings at a time, to sweep over the coastal belt of occupied Europe, or to escort small formations of Blenheim or Stirling bombers to bomb targets within range. Both operations were designed to tempt up the Luftwaffe fighters to give battle in the hope of so weakening the units still in the west as to require withdrawals from the new front in Russia. Coastal Command bombers were also escorted to attack coastal shipping in the Channel, the North Sea, and in the coastal ports, while in cloudy conditions pairs and quartettes of fighters flew nuisance raids –'Rhubarbs'– looking for targets of opportunity to strafe.

In fact the Luftwaffe was able to engage or not at will, usually with the advantage of height and sun. Early in 1941 the excellent Messerschmitt Bf 109F fighter had been introduced, which was the equal of the Spitfire VB, and superior to earlier types. Late in the year came the new Focke-Wulf Fw 190, superior to all British fighters then in service. It was a rough time for the Allied units, and losses were high for little return. The pilots believed that they were taking a toll of the Germans equal to, or higher than their own losses – a belief that was tacitly allowed to prevail for reasons of morale. The truth was sobering, as the British High Command knew well; losses were in fact far higher than those suffered by the Germans – a break-even was an excellent result!

Against this background, it is not surprising that the fresh young Canadians did not accomplish a great deal during this initial period. Indeed by the end of 1941 all five squadrons then operational had claimed just 22 confirmed victories between them. By October 401, 411 and 412 Squadrons had all converted to Spitfire VBs, 401 Squadron moving to the premier fighter station at Biggin Hill. Here, however, the quality of the opposition was hammered home to the unit on 27 October, when during a sweep the Luftwaffe inflicted losses on it of five shot down and two damaged; against this shattering defeat, claims amounted to only one probable and two damaged.

Meanwhile 402 Squadron had withdrawn to become one of the first Hurribomber units, its Hurricane IIBs being modified to carry a 250lb bomb beneath each wing. In this guise it resumed operations on 1 November with an eight-aircraft attack on Berck-sur-Mer airfield in Normandy. The Spitfires continued their activities over France, claiming the odd victory, but continuing to suffer heavily and frequently.

Further fighter units were now appearing, however, 416 Squadron forming at Peterhead, Scotland, in November and 417 Squadron at Charmy Down during the same month. Both had converted to

Spitfire VBs by March 1942, as did 402 Squadron, which as a result ceased its fighter-bomber activities; in that same month, however, 417 Squadron stood down again prior to departure for service in the Middle East. Six RCAF Spitfire Squadrons were operating during the spring and early summer of 1942, but 2 June saw the worst single loss ever to be suffered by a Canadian fighter unit. On the morning of this day 403 Squadron was led off on a sweep over France in company with several RAF squadrons, the unit being led by its new New Zealand commanding officer, Battle of Britain ace Sqn Ldr A C 'Al' Deere. The squadron suffered a disastrous 'bounce', which sent seven Spitfires down, only one pilot being seen to bale out; an eighth was hard-hit and crash-landed on return, only four landing back at base. The unit was at once sent north to rest and recuperate, while a few weeks later Deere was replaced by Sqn Ldr Les Ford, a rising RCAF 'star' who had served with several of the other units already.

The last RCAF fighter squadron to be formed in the UK, 421, had been 'born' at Digby during April, and by mid-summer 1942 all seven units were available for action. In July 401 Squadron exchanged its Spitfire VBs for the very latest Mark IXs, which were at last a match for the Fw 190s; 402 Squadron was similarly re-equipped during August. It was August which saw the main event of the year for the Fighter Command units, when on 19th landings were made at Dieppe on the French coast to test invasion techniques and German reaction to them. Operation 'Jubilee' was to a considerable extent a Canadian effort on the ground, while in the air the largest force ever gathered by Fighter Command attempted to maintain an air 'umbrella' over the landings. In this the fighters were extremely successful, but at the cost of the heaviest losses in a single day ever suffered by the Command – over 100.

All the Canadian Spitfire squadrons bar 421 were to take part, joined by elements of both RCAF army co-operation units, and at first light by the intruders from 418 Squadron. A Boston from the latter unit was the first casualty of the day to an Fw 190, but thereafter the Spitfire units were over the port in a constant stream.

Above: Hugh Godefroy of 401 Squadron seen soon after the award of his DFC in 1943. One of the RCAF's great leaders, he was to lead 127 Wing in early 1944, adding a DSO and a Bar to his DFC.
Below: The Bolton-Paul Defiant was an expensive failure as a fighter and was relegated to the night fighter role.

Each unit flew at least three squadron-strength patrols, several undertaking a fourth. Twice formations of Luftwaffe bombers were encountered – Do 217s by 401 Squadron, Ju 88s by 416 Squadron – but while many claims for damaged against these were made, none could be claimed destroyed by the Canadians. By the end of the day in nine engagements the RCAF Spitfire pilots had claimed a total of 6½ confirmed, 6 probables and 20 damaged against a loss of nine Spitfires and six damaged.

Gradually, as the pilots became used to the new Spitfire IXs and started to alter their tactics from the basically defensive ones employed with the Spitfire VBs against the superior Fw 190s, a little more success was achieved, but it remained an uphill battle for the rest of the year. It has to be admitted that 1942 had brought little more impressive results than 1941. In the full year the total of confirmed victories for all seven units amounted to just 35½, while losses had been substantially higher – including several of the new Mark IXs. The only pilot of any note to appear had been Plt Off Donald Morrison who was RCAF top-scorer for the 1941-2 period with four and three shared confirmed, three and one shared probable and five damaged. However, he was shot down on 8 November 1942 and badly wounded, becoming a prisoner of war.

Fortunately, the tide was about to turn in the Canadians' favor,

due to a number of reasons and changed circumstances. During 1941 and most of 1942 the squadrons had flown individually as components of RAF Wings, but toward the end of the latter year they began to be formed into two-squadron RCAF Wings within No 11 Group, based upon Kenley and Redhill. Immediately after the Dieppe fiasco, large numbers of RAF squadrons were withdrawn for service in northwest Africa, where the Anglo-American Operation 'Torch' landings took place on 8 November. As a result the offensive over western Europe devolved more upon the Commonwealth and foreign national squadrons which remained based in the United Kingdom. Around the end of 1942/early 1943 some experienced RCAF pilots began returning for second tours, and their leadership as squadron, flight, and section commanders, coupled with the growing availability of Spitfire IXs was to have a remarkable effect on results achieved in 1943.

At the same time the US heavy bomber offensive had just begun, initially requiring escort to the limit of the Spitfire's range – at least until US escort fighters became available in sufficient quantities to take over the task. In Bomber Command, too, the availability of numbers of more potent light and medium bombers, followed in due course by USAAF medium bombers, provided more opportunities to escort raids of a more sustained and damaging nature. All this

Below: Brand-new Spitfire IX (BS306 'A') of 402 Squadron at Kenley in late 1942.
Bottom left: Lloyd Chadburn DSO*, DFC, commanded 402 Squadron in early 1943, and then led the Digby Wing. He was killed over Normandy in a mid-air collision on 13 June 1944.

increased activity now at last led to a growing reinforcement of the west by Luftwaffe fighters from other fronts, while the demands of the expanding war zones were thinning out the ranks of the highly experienced older German fighter pilots and bringing in growing numbers of new entrants.

The change was not sudden, and there was much hard fighting still to come – but the seeds were there. Throughout 1943 the squadrons alternated on a rota basis between the Midlands and the No 11 Group bases, usually swapping aircraft so that those engaged in daily sweeps flew the Mark IXs, and those involved in convoy patrols and training employed the Mark VBs. In the spring a young RAF pilot, Wg Cdr D E 'Johnny' Johnson, was posted in to lead the Kenley Wing. Johnson's career to date had not been particularly distinguished as a fighter pilot; he had claimed six and two shared victories during the past 21 months – but he exuded leadership, and his promotion had been rapid. His personality complemented the Canadians to perfection, and the growing success of the Kenley Wing was to be inextricably linked with him. Indeed, he was soon to be invited to wear the RCAF's 'Canada' flashes on the shoulders of his uniform – a unique honor at this time for an RAF officer.

During April Johnson led the Wing, comprised at this time of 403 and 416 Squadrons, to their first big successes, 17 victories being claimed for only three losses during three operations in this one month. May proved to be another successful month, but June was marred by the loss to flak of Wg Cdr Les Ford, ex 403 Squadron commander, and newly promoted Wing Leader at Digby. Ford had raised his personal score to six before leaving the unit – one of the first RCAF aces. His place was taken by another leading Canadian pilot of this period, Lloyd Chadburn, previously commanding officer of 402 Squadron. All units were in action at various times

Bottom: Sqn Ldr L S 'Les' Ford DFC* (center), was the most successful RCAF fighter pilot of 1942. He was killed by ships' antiaircraft fire leading the Digby Wing on 4 June 1943.

during the summer, but 4 September saw the end of Johnson's tour when he led 402 Squadron to a four-nil victory over Le Touquet. His place was now taken by Hugh Godefroy, recently of 403 Squadron.

During the latter part of the year the Digby Wing also obtained some successes over the North Sea, but in October moves were made preparatory to the official formation of 2nd Tactical Air Force. Ready for this event, 401, 411 and 412 Squadrons moved to Biggin Hill, which became known as 126 Airfield, where all three units reconverted to Spitfire IXs. The ex-Malta pilot, R W 'Buck' McNair, was posted from 421 Squadron to lead this new Wing. At the same time Kenley, where 403 and 421 Squadrons were based, became 127 Airfield, both bases initially forming an all-embracing 17 Fighter Wing – although each airfield continued to have its own Wing Leader. Operations continued meanwhile under control of No 11 Group, as the units began working up for the mobile tactical role in support of the armies in the forthcoming invasion of Europe.

While the Canadians' main opponents had continued to be the German fighters, on occasion other types had appeared. Late in the year a Ju 87, a Ju 88, a Do 217 and a Do 24 rescue flying boat were among aircraft shot down. Results in 1943 had indeed been very different, the RCAF Spitfire units claiming more than 135 victories; 403 Squadron had been the most successful with 50, while 421 Squadron had claimed 35. The most successful pilot had been Wg Cdr Johnson, who had claimed 13 and five shared during his six months at the head of the Kenley Wing, but by the end of the year ten RCAF pilots had claimed five or more victories over Western Europe since the initiation of operations early in 1941. The most successful was 'Buck' McNair, who had claimed nine – one before going to Malta and eight since his return – to raise his personal score to 17. Flt Lt H D MacDonald, DFC and Bar, had claimed seven and one shared before his death in action on 30 November 1943, while Wg Cdr Godefroy and Sqn Ldr Geoff Northcott of 401 Squadron each had seven victories. Wg Cdr Chadburn had five and four shared, plus six and one shared probables and seven damaged, and Flt Lt R A Buckham of 421 Squadron six and one shared. The Canadians' fortunes had certainly changed, but greater things were still to come.

Below: A Vickers Wellington II of 405 Squadron being bombed up and refuelled for a raid.

Night Fighters

While three night fighter squadrons had been formed by mid-1941, all remained based in northern England and the Midlands for many months. Here, following the departure of the Luftwaffe to the Russian front in June, there were few sustained alerts, and successful interceptions were rare. The first was made during the night of 1 September 1941 by Flg Off R C Fumerton of 406 Squadron, while on 1 November Wg Cdr P Y Davoud of 409 Squadron claimed a Do 217 in one of the Beaufighter IIs to which the unit had soon converted. 'Moose' Fumerton was to become the RCAF's outstanding night fighter, while Paul Davoud was one of the greatest night fighter unit commanders.

410 Squadron also received Beaufighter IIs during March 1942, but in June the other two units began exchanging theirs for radial-engined Mark VIs. These brought more combats for the Midlands-based 409 Squadron, but no conclusive successes, four probables being claimed during the summer. Meanwhile a fourth night unit had been formed at Digby during November 1941, which began operational flying during March 1942. This was 418 Squadron, which was to undertake intruder operations over France, equipped initially with Douglas Boston IIIs. These sorties were of a particularly hazardous nature, and losses were quite heavy, but by the end of the year two German aircraft had been claimed destroyed over their own airfields.

Thus by the close of 1942 four RCAF night fighter units were in existence – 406 at Scorton, 409 at Coleby Grange, 410 at Digby, where it had converted to Mosquito IIs in October, and 418 at Bradwell Bay. All had been in existence for over a year, but total achievement by the whole force to date amounted to just 15 confirmed and six probable victories; indeed not until 22 January 1943 was 410 Squadron to claim its first success. In March 1943 406 Squadron moved to Middle Wallop in No 10 Group's area in the south of England, while 409 Squadron moved to Acklington in the north and 410 Squadron took its place at Coleby Grange; 418 Squadron moved to Ford. All four units claimed during the month, March

bringing the best total to date with three Do 217s and a Ju 88 credited to the Canadians; however, it was to be a fairly 'lean' year again for defensive operations, 406 Squadron gaining no further victories, and 409 only one more. With its new Mosquitos, however, 410 Squadron now undertook some offensive 'Ranger' operations over the North Sea, and was able as a result to record eight successes; four of these were credited to Flg Off R D Schultz, who claimed three Do 217s in a single night on 10 December, by which time the unit had moved to Hunsdon in No 11 Group's southeast England area. Mosquito VIs had supplemented the Mark IIs during the summer, but at the end of the year Mark XIIIs were received with updated centimetric radar.

During the spring 418 Squadron had also begun to supplement its Bostons with Mosquito VIs, although the older aircraft were not finally phased out until September. The new equipment allowed the unit to begin long-ranging intruding sorties by day up into the Luftwaffe's training areas in Denmark and North Germany, and in this new role great success was to be achieved. Up to the end of August 1943 the squadron had claimed only nine victories in the air, but by the end of that same year this total had risen to 20. During the first five months of 1944 the unit was to range far and wide, and by the time the invasion fleet sailed for Normandy, 57 further air victories had been claimed, plus 46 destroyed on the ground, making 418 Squadron at this stage the most successful of all RCAF fighter units. Among its most successful pilots at the time were Sqn Ldr H D Cleveland, Flt Lt D A MacFadyen, Flg Off J T Caine, Sqn Ldr R A Kipp, Sqn Ldr C C Scherf, an Australian, and Lt J F Luma, a member of the USAAF; from June 1943 the unit had enjoyed the leadership of Paul Davoud.

In March 406 Squadron moved south to Exeter where in the next three months 12 victories and two probables were claimed, one of these by Wg Cdr Fumerton, who had returned to command the unit after service in the Middle East, so that he had claimed the first and the last of his 13 victories with the unit. During this period the squadron converted to Mosquito XIIs. 410 Squadron, now at Castle Camps, continued to enjoy success, claiming a further eight victims during the first five months of 1944, while 409 Squadron, although

Above right: Canada's leading night fighter ace, Wg Cdr R C 'Moose' Fumerton DFC, who was credited with 13 air victories and one on the ground.

Above: Flt Lt M A Cybulski (rt) and his radar operator, L H A Cadbrook, by the scorched tail of their 410 Squadron Mosquito night fighter after flying 250 miles back from Holland following a combat with a Dornier 217 bomber which they shot down; this combat occurred during the night of 26 September 1943.
Below: A Hawker Typhoon IB fighter-bomber of 439 Squadron (JP401) landing on a forward airstrip in North Germany in early 1945.

seeing no action during this period, completed conversion to Mosquito XIIIs.

Following receipt of the Mosquitos, 409 Squadron joined 2nd TAF, as did 410 Squadron, both units joining 148 Wing at Hunsdon, and then West Malling. From here 410 Squadron made the first authorized use of Mark VIII AI radar over enemy territory during an intruder sortie on 18 May. When the invasion began in June, 409 remained in 148 wing with 29 Squadron, RAF, and a squadron of new Griffon-engined Spitfire XIVs, but 410 moved to 141 Wing at Hartford Bridge, joining 264 Squadron, RAF, and another Spitfire XIV unit; later in the month the squadron would move to join 147 Wing at Zeals. Operations over the beachhead area were continuous, each unit claiming 11 victories during June, while in July 409 claimed eight for two losses, and 410 six. Remaining on defense of the home ports, 406 Squadron claimed four victories in two nights during these two months, but was then stood down to convert to Mosquito XXXs. 410 Squadron also received these aircraft, while 409 became the first night fighter unit to move to France, flying over to B17 landing ground at Carpiquet on 25 August. Despite conversion, 410 Squadron continued to be active throughout the month, and each unit again claimed 11 victories.

Poorer weather and the German retreat brought fewer targets during September, 409 Squadron moving forward to Saint Andre, while 410 Squadron also moved across to France late in the month, initially to Amiens. Victories remained much scarcer during the rest of 1944, although during late November four Ju 88G night fighters were shot down by 410 Squadron, three of them in one night by another USAAF pilot, Lt A A Harrington, to raise his personal score to seven. The Ardennes operations in December brought more activity, 16 victories being claimed during the latter part of the month to bring the scores since the invasion to 38 for 409 Squadron and 41 for 410; losses generally had been very light – not more than half a dozen aircraft.

Meanwhile 418 Squadron had continued its intruder operations since June, but had been much involved during the summer in intercepting the V-1 flying bombs now menacing southern England. No less than 68 of these missiles were shot down, 19 of them by Sqn Ldr R Bannock, who had claimed five of the further 26 victories over piloted aircraft credited to the unit by 1 November; 27 more were claimed destroyed on the ground. At that point the squadron was posted to No 2 Group in 2nd TAF, joining 605 Squadron, RAF, to form 136 Wing at Hartford Bridge. From now on it became involved entirely in operations over the Continent against ground targets, and no further victories in the air were to be claimed.

Its place in the intruder role was taken by 406 Squadron, which moved to Manston with its new Mosquito XXXs and at once began undertaking nocturnal standing patrols over the Luftwaffe's night fighter airfields. Several of the more successful 418 Squadron pilots, including Bannock, Caine and MacFadyen, were posted to the squadron for these duties, and much success was to be obtained from December 1944 onward, 23 aerial victories and nine destroyed on the ground being claimed by the end of the war, Bannock and MacFadyen each adding four more aerial victories, and the latter another two on the ground. Meanwhile 418 Squadron found its new duties costly. On 22 February 1945 No 2 Group's Mosquitos undertook wide-ranging daylight attacks on German transport targets, all Wings suffering heavy losses to Flak. Four of 418's Mosquitos were lost, including that flown by Wg Cdr J Wickett, the commanding officer; this brought losses in the month to a record seven aircraft. During mid-March 136 Wing moved over from England to Coxyde in Belgium, and from there to Volkel in Holland a month later.

The offensives of the British 21st Army Group in Northwest Europe which began during February 1945 brought more action for 409 and 410 Squadrons, which also managed to intercept a number of V-1s which were being air-launched against Antwerp. In April 148 Wing moved to German soil, 409 Squadron going to B108 airfield at Rheine, and from here a last flurry of interceptions took place late in the month, three Ju 52s, two Ju 87s and an Fw 190 being

shot down during the night of 23/24th, while three more aircraft were claimed next night to rise the squadron's total to 57 since D-Day. During the month in 410 Squadron, three victories had been claimed, all by Flt Lt R D Schultz, now on his second tour, to bring this unit's total to 56 since D-Day, and Schultz's personal total to eight.

Total night victories for RCAF night fighter squadrons amounted to 186 (406 Squadron 50; 409 Squadron 62; 410 Squadron 74), while 418 Squadron had claimed 102 in the air and 75 on the ground. Most successful Canadian night fighter pilots in Western Europe had been R A Kipp (10½ air, 2 ground); R Bannock (9 air, 2 ground, 19 V-1s); R D Schultz (8 air); D A MacFadyen (7 air, 5 ground, 5 V-1s); J T Caine (5 air, 15 ground). All four squadrons were soon disbanded; 410 Squadron on 9 June, 409 on 1 July, 406 on 1 September and 418 on 7 September.

The Reconnaissance Squadrons

It will be recalled that by late summer of 1941 two RCAF army co-operation squadrons were available, both of which had been equipped mainly with Curtiss Tomahawk fighters. These aircraft were not considered as fully suitable for operations over Western Europe, and were employed only as interim equipment. However, in November some operations were flown by 400 Squadron over the Channel and French coast, but on one such on 13 December both aircraft involved failed to return. Operations ceased again at the start of 1942 as both units awaited re-equipment with the new North American Mustang I low-level reconnaissance fighter, the first of these reaching 400 Squadron in May and 414 Squadron during the following month.

The Dieppe landings – Operation 'Jubilee' – occurred on 19 August, before either squadron was fully operational on the Mustang, but an army co-operation composite wing was temporarily formed, and both units contributed aircraft and pilots to this, flying a number of sorties over the port. Here 400 lost one aircraft, while Flg Off Hollis Hills, an American member of 414 Squadron, claimed an Fw 190 shot down for the Mustang's first victory of the war. Soon after Dieppe both squadrons were fully operational, flying a variety of intruder missions over the European coast in twos and fours, as well as shipping reconnaissances and other such missions – under the codenames 'Rhubarb', 'Jim Crow', 'Instep' and 'Lagoon'. On occasions enemy aircraft of various types were met, and by the end of October 1943 400 Squadron had claimed ten of these shot down, including two Messerschmitt Bf 110 night fighters during night

intruder sorties in August, while 414 Squadron had claimed a further three in the air and two on the ground. Meanwhile on 1 January 1943 a third squadron of Mustangs had been formed, 430, and this began operations similar to the other two during May. These activities could be costly, flown as they were at low altitude in the face of considerable light Flak, and subject to frequent interceptions by Fw 190s. By the end of 1943 400 and 414 Squadrons had each lost eight aircraft on operations during the year, and 430 Squadron a further five.

During the year Army Co-operation Command was disbanded and its squadrons transferred to Fighter Command pending formation of the new tactical air force which was to support the forthcoming invasion. As plans for the latter were advanced, exercises were flown with the army during 1943, while in the fall cameras were fitted to many aircraft, and reconnaissance missions began, to record in detail the coastal defenses.

In November 2nd Tactical Air Force was officially formed and all three squadrons were transferred to it, although initially operations and bases remained unchanged. On 2 November Flg Offs R O Brown and G Wonnacott of 414 Squadron on a 'Rhubarb' over the Cambrai area, strafed four trains and then shot down two Fw 190s, while a little over a week later two pilots of 400 Squadron engaged

three Me 210s, claiming two shot down and the third probable – the last aerial victories for this squadron. On 28 January 1944 four 414 Squadron aircraft achieved further success when two Bf 109s were claimed shot down by Flt Lt G W Burroughes and Flg Off Wonnacott, following which this pair shot down one of two Ar 96 trainers, the other being shot down by Flg Off R O Brown, although the latter failed to return from this sortie. During January 400 Squadron converted 'A' Flight to Spitfire XIs and 'B' Flight to Mosquito XVIs – both unarmed photo-reconnaissance types. Reconnaissance operations continued throughout the spring of 1944, 414 and 430 Squadrons also attending armament practice camps, while the former also attended a course at the Royal Navy's Naval Bombardment Spotting School. In April both squadrons moved to Odiham and flew frequent operations with formations of Spitfires and Typhoons which were attacking coastal targets, the Mustangs photographing the results. In June the three squadrons formed 39 (Recce) Wing with 168 Squadron, RAF; by now 400 Squadron had become fully equipped with Spitfire XIs, and was flying many high altitude reconnaissance missions.

During the first days of the invasion of Normandy, 414 Squadron was involved in spotting for the guns of the ships supporting the landings, but thereafter both Mustang squadrons were greatly in-

volved in tactical reconnaissnce sorties for the army. Ranging over enemy supply and reinforcement lines at low level, the Mustangs were at high risk, and by the end of the month ten aircraft had been lost, including that flown by 414 Squadron's commanding officer, Sqn Ldr S H Stover, who baled out. At the end of the month the Wing began moving to French soil, from where operations continued, although more Luftwaffe fighters were encountered during July and August. While three more Mustangs were lost, the pilots frequently were able to fight back, and in this period three Fw 190s were claimed in return

Early in August 414 Squadron started converting to Spitfire IXs, beginning operations again in mid-September, initially attached to a fighter wing. 400 Squadron's high-flying Spitfire XIs were frequently intercepted by German fighters during the fall, but generally managed to use their height and speed advantage to escape – even when intercepted by Me 262 jets, as began increasingly to happen at this time. During November 430 Squadron was selected to receive new Griffon-engined Spitfire XIVs, and operations with

Above: North American Mustang I (AM251) of 414 Squadron in 1943. Below: Westland Lysander III army cooperation aircraft of 400 Squadron at Odiham in 1940.

the Mustang began to run down, although by the end of the year this unit would have lost 17 of the older aircraft to various operational causes since the invasion.

After a relatively static fall, the German Ardennes Offensive brought much action during December for all squadrons. Spitfires of 414 Squadron flew 36 sorties on Christmas Eve, twice being engaged by large formations of Bf 109s. On the first occasion Flt Lt D I Hall claimed two shot down, while on the second, three and a probable were claimed by Flt Lt W Sawers. 430's new Spitfire XIVs on occasion flew escort to 400's Mark XIs, and on 31 December six of the new aircraft were flown to Y-32 airfield in the US sector of the front. Dawn on 1 January 1945 brought the famous Luftwaffe New Year's Day attack on Allied airfields in Europe. 400 Squadron's aircraft were caught parked in straight lines at Eindhoven where five were destroyed and four badly damaged, while 430 Squadron lost seven aircraft – three of them old Mustangs – and 414 Squadron had four of its Spitfires badly damaged. Several pilots from the latter unit were in the air, and two of these claimed four German fighters shot down; three of them fell to Gordon Wonnacott, now the commanding officer, who thus became the first ace of the reconnaissance wing, and received a Bar to his DFC.

Soon after this attack, 414 Squadron moved up to Kluis where it was much involved supporting the army during the spring fighting in the Reichswald Forest, and in April this unit began re-equipping with Spitfire XIVBs, featuring cut-down rear fuselages and 'tear-drop' cockpit hoods. On 10 April the Wing moved to B108 airfield at Rheine on German soil, and here on the 15th Flt Lt W M Middleton shot down an Fw 190 for 430 Squadron's second victory. In a final engagement on 2 May, Flt Lt D I Hall, DFC, shot down three Fw 190s and a Bf 109, and damaged one of each while Sqn Ldr J B Prendergast, DFC, claimed two more Fw 190s to raise 414's victory total to 28½; with seven personal victories, Hall became the unit's second ace. Following the end of hostilities the three units remained in Germany with the occupation forces until early August 1945, when all three were disbanded at Lüneburg.

Bomber Command

Following the formation of the first two bomber squadrons, two more were to follow before the end of 1941. 419 Squadron formed at Mildenhall in December, under the command of a notable Canadian bomber pilot, Wg Cdr John 'Moose' Fulton, DSO, DFC, AFC; equipped with Wellington ICs, the unit operated within No 3 Group. During the same month 420 Squadron was formed further south at Waddington as a No 5 Group Hampden unit. Thus at the start of 1942 RCAF bomber strength stood as follows:

No 3 Group

419 Squadron	Mildenhall	7 Wellington IC non-operational

No 4 Group

405 Squadron	Pocklington	18 Wellington II

No 5 Group

408 Squadron	Syerston	26 Hampden	
420 Squadron	Waddington	20 Hampden	non-operational

This small force was nonetheless active, 68 RCAF bombers taking part in the first 1000 bomber raid on Cologne in May 1942. During the previous month 405 Squadron had become the first to begin conversion to the new four-engined 'heavies', when Handley-Page Halifax IIs were received. Similar equipment reached 408 and 419 Squadrons during October, but this month saw 405 Squadron being loaned to Coastal Command on a temporary basis to patrol over the Bay of Biscay during the sailing of the Allied convoys for the Anglo-American 'Torch' landings in northwest Africa; the unit would return to Bomber Command control in March 1943. During August 1942 420 Squadron had left No 5 Group, moving to North Yorkshire to re-equip with Wellingtons and join No 4 Group.

Meanwhile during June 1942 425 Squadron had been formed at

Dishforth, Yorkshire, as a French Canadian unit – the first such to be formed, carrying the name 'Alouette'. Equipped with Wellington IIIs, this unit served initially in No 4 Group, where it was joined in October by two more new Canadian Wellington units, 424 Squadron at Topcliffe and 426 Squadron at Dishforth. This was only the beginning of a massive expansion of the RCAF bomber force, for during the next month four more units appeared – all with Wellingtons and all in north Yorkshire or County Durham.

This tremendous increase in what was to become Canada's major contribution to the air war preceded the formation of a new all-Canadian bomber group within Bomber Command – a unique formation which was totally funded by the Canadian government. The Headquarters of No 6 (RCAF) Group was set up at Linton-on-Ouse in October 1942, the Group formally coming into existence on 1 January 1943. Seven RAF stations were initially handed over, these including Middleton St George, Croft, Leeming, Topcliffe, Dalton and Dishforth, all in Yorkshire, and all already in use by RCAF units. In addition, a seventh airfield was Skipton-on-Swale, which was then still under construction. The Group was also given control of 1659 Heavy Conversion Unit, which was already in use by the Canadian units. The new Group's first operation was flown during the night of 3/4 January when six Wellingtons of 427 Squadron laid mines off the Frisian Islands. By the start of March 1943, when 405 Squadron returned 'to the fold', No 6 Group had nine squadrons on hand, and RCAF bomber strength had grown nearly threefold:

No 4 Group

429 Squadron	East Moor	11 Wellington III, 3 Wellington X
431 Squadron	Burn	20 Wellington X

No 6 (RCAF) Group

405 Squadron	Topcliffe	21 Halifax
408 Squadron	Leeming	18 Halifax
419 Squadron	Middleton St George	18 Halifax
420 Squadron	Middleton St George	10 Wellington III, 8 Wellington X
424 Squadron	Topcliffe	10 Wellington III, 8 Wellington X
425 Squadron	Dishforth	17 Wellington III
426 Squadron	Dishforth	17 Wellington III, 2 Wellington X
427 Squadron	Croft	11 Wellington III, 4 Wellington X
428 Squadron	Dalton	12 Wellington III, 6 Wellington X

During April, however, the Group temporarily lost 420, 424 and 425 Squadrons when these units were detached to Africa to aid in the forthcoming invasions of Sicily and Italy. During May, however, a new unit, 432 Squadron, formed with Wellingtons, followed in June by 434 Squadron which received Halifax Vs from the start. Halifaxes were becoming available in greater quantities at this time, 427 Squadron having moved to Leeming during May to convert to Mark Vs, while during June 428 Squadron also converted to this version, followed in July by 431 Squadron. This squadron at last joined No 6 Group – the last No 4 Group unit to do so, as 429 Squadron had already been incorporated during June, when its East Moor base and the new airfield at Wombleton were also transferred to the Group. Other new equiment arrived in June, when 426 Squadron re-equipped with Lancaster IIs – the first Lancasters in the Group. This was followed by similar equipment for 405 and 408 Squadrons during August, and for 432 Squadron in October. Meanwhile in September the last new bomber unit to be formed, 433 Squadron, was brought into existence, although its new Halifax IIIs were not to become available until November, and no operations would be flown until January 1944. 429 Squadron at last converted from its Wellingtons to Halifax IIs in September, but in November 428 Squadron exchanged its Halifax Vs for this unit's aircraft.

In June 1943 the main Linton-on-Ouse airfield had been transferred to the RCAF together with its subsidiary station, Tholthorpe,

which was still under construction. No 6 Group now organized the first of three area sub-groupings for administrative convenience. Each was based upon a major airfield and included its subsidiary airfields. This first sub-grouping, known as 62 (Beaver) Base, covered the southern area of the Group's geographical zone. Linton-on-Ouse was the main base, with East Moor and Tholthorpe as the sub-stations. Subsequently in May 1944 63 and 64 Bases would be created; 63 Base covered the central geogrphical area, centered upon Leeming, with Skipton-on-Swale as the sub-station, while in the northern area 64 Base was located at Middleton St George, with Croft as sub-station. 61 Base was also formed to comprise the training units, centered on Topcliffe, with Wombleton and Dishforth as sub-stations, but later in 1944 these airfields with 1659, 1664 and 1666 Heavy Conversion Units reverted to the RAF Training Group.

No 6 Group was never to have all RCAF bomber units under its direct control at one time, for even as 431 Squadron at last joined the fold, 405 – the original RCAF bomber unit – was posted to No 8 (Pathfinder) Group to become one of the target locating and marking units of that elite force. For administration purposes it remained under No 6 Group control, but not for operations. Toward the end of the year 405 became the first unit to receive some of the new Canadian-built Lancaster Xs which were to appear in growing quantities during the later months of the war. The Halifax III had become standardized as No 6 Group equipment, however, and when 420, 424 and 425 Squadrons returned from their Mediterranean detachment at the end of 1943, they were all to be re-equipped with these aircraft before resuming operations early in the new year. 427 Squadron exchanged Halifax Vs for these aircraft in January 1944, while in Febuary 432 followed suit, as did 429 and 431 Squadrons during March, and 434 in May. 431 Squadron also received a few Mark VIIs. Early in 1944 419 Squadron exchanged its Halifax IIs for new Canadian Lancaster Xs, but soon afterward 408 Squadron gave up its Lancaster IIs for Halifax IIIs, so that by mid-summer all but one of the Group's squadrons operated these aircraft, steadily supplemented by more Mark VIIs.

During February 1944, after a year of operations, the Group's AOC, AVM G E Brookes, was replaced by one of the leading World War I fighter aces, AVM C M MacEwen, and he was to command until the end of the war. The final addition came in July 1944 when 415 Squadron was transferred from Coastal to Bomber Command, re-equipping with Halifax IIIs and moving to East Moor from where it flew its first bombing sorties over Germany during a raid on Hamburg on the night of 28/29 July.

The Canadian contribution had reached its zenith in 1944, during which year the Group suffered the lowest percentage losses of any of Bomber Command's four-engined formations. During 1943, the first year of operations, 7355 sorties were flown by No 6 Group aircraft, which dropped 13,630 tons of bombs for the loss of 340 aircraft. In 1944 sorties rose to 25,353, and bomb tonnage to 86,503, but losses were contained at 377. The biggest raid undertaken by the Group occurred on the night of 6/7 October 1944 when 293 Canadian Lancasters and Halifaxes raided Dortmund, only two being lost. A week later 25 percent of the total Bomber Command effort was provided for two attacks on Duisburg, one by day and one by night. 501 sorties were flown by No 6 Group aircraft during these attacks, for the loss of five. Increasingly after the summer of 1944, Bomber Command's heavies operated by day over Germany in the face of the much reduced fighter opposition then to be found. This backfired badly only once, but it was No 6 Group which took the brunt of an interception by Me 262 jets during an attack on Hamburg on 31 March 1945; heavy losses were sustained.

By the end of the war the Group had flown 40,822 operational sorties in a little under two and a half years, to drop 126,122 tons of bombs at a cost of 814 aircraft. The combined totals for all the squadrons were higher, of course, because of the earlier service of several, and of the operations of others outside the Group. All but the last few to be formed flew at least 3000 sorties each, some of the older units achieving well over 4000. Losses frequently had been heavy, and 419 Squadron alone had lost 129 aircraft – about five times its normal strength! Most of the 8000 plus decorations awarded to members of the RCAF went to Bomber Command, 408 Squadron for instance receiving 210 awards, while 419 Squadron received four DSOs, 150 DFCs and three Bars, 35 DFMs and a Military Cross – plus the Group's only VC, awarded posthumously after the war to a mid-upper gunner, Plt Off Andrew Mynarski, who died on 12 June 1944. During a raid on Cambrai Mynarski's aircraft was shot down in flames by fighters. He made a valiant attempt to free the trapped rear gunner until his own clothing was ablaze, and only then did he bale out, dying of his burns. Miraculously, the rear gunner survived to return and report Mynarski's selfless courage at the end of the war.

During 1944 the Halifaxes had gradually begun to give way to Lancasters, 428 Squadron converting to Lancaster Xs in June, followed by 431 Squadron in October and 434 in December. In January 1945 424 and 433 Squadrons received Lancaster Is, while in March 427 and 429 re-equipped with a mixture of Mark Is and IIIs. By mid-April the final wartime strength of No 6 Group stood at 40 Halifax IIIs, 67 Halifax VIIs, 90 Lancaster Is and IIIs, and 101 Lancaster Xs – a total of 298 aircraft available for operations. Within days of the European war ending, 415 and 432 Squadrons were disbanded. Several other units, notably 427, 433 and 434, were involved in flying liberated prisoners of war to England, while on the close of hostilities 408, 420 and 425 Squadrons all converted to Lancaster Xs. In June 1945 these units joined 405, 419, 428, 431 and 434 Squadrons in flying home to Canada where they were to form the nucleus of the RCAF contribution to 'Tiger Force' to take part in the war against Japan. By this time 430 Canadian-built Lancaster Xs, with which all these units were equipped, had been built.

The other five units remained in Britain, 426 Squadron being converted to Liberators to operate in the transport role on the Far East run. In August 1945 this unit began ferrying troops back from India, following the conclusion of hostilities with Japan, until its disbandment in December. Also in August 424, 427, 429 and 433 Squadrons were all transferred to the RAF's No 1 Group for transport duties, flying troops from Italy to England. During October 424 and 433 were disbanded, while in May 1946 the last two units were similarly stood down.

Coastal Command

As in other Commands, RCAF involvement in Coastal was to cover all aspects of the work of that most variegated Command. Before 1941 was over 404 Squadron's Blenheim fighters were patrolling over shipping off Scotland, 407 Squadron's Hudsons were attacking German shipping off the North Sea coasts, and the Catalinas of 413 Squadron were involved in anti-submarine patrols. Late in the year the Blenheims were involved in providing cover for the Commando raid on Vaagso, in Norway, and were engaged in combat with opposing Messerchmitts, claiming one probable without loss. The activities of 407 Squadron proved somewhat hazardous, however, and six Hudsons were to be lost during the last quarter of the year. In January 1942 the unit began operating by night instead. After a short rest in February, a detachment was sent to St Eval in Cornwall from where patrols were flown over the ships involved in the Commando attack on St Nazaire, France. A move back to the east, to Bircham Newton, brought renewed North Sea operations, again at high cost, four Hudsons being lost in April, while on 15 May eleven aircraft took part in a costly attack on a convoy off the Dutch coast. While three ships were left in flames, four aircraft failed to return and two more crashed on landing.

Meanwhile during May 413 Squadron had been despatched to the Far East, but in the month that followed 415 Squadron commenced its torpedo-bombing operations, having converted to Hampdens for this role at the start of the month. Operations were flown initially over the Biscay area where during May the first attack was made on a 6000 ton freighter; this was claimed damaged, although one Hampden was lost. In June the unit joined 407 Squadron on the east coast, operating over the North Sea from North Coates. Like the Hudson crews, the Hampdens found conditions here dangerous as the coastal convoys they were attacking usually included heavily

Above: Mosquito FB VI of 418 Squadron. This unit operated with distinction in the intruder role, first with Fighter Command and later as a part of 2nd TAF.
Below: Bristol Beaufighter rocket-fighters of Coastal Command, operated by 404 Squadron in 1944; note the black and white Invasion stripes.

armed Flak ships, and often fighter escorts; four Hampdens were lost in the first month.

Coastal Command was requested to provide aircraft for some of the first 1000 bomber raids during 1942, in order to bring Bomber Command's maximum effort up to the desired numbers, and on 25 June Hudsons of 407 Squadron took part in the attack on Bremen. Shortly thereafter this unit moved again to the west of England, operating over the Western Approaches and Biscay until early 1943, when conversion to Wellington XIs and XIIs took place for a full change of role to anti-submarine patrol.

404 Squadron was operating over the same area at the turn of the year, having converted from Blenheims to Beaufighter IIs late in 1942. In April 1943 this unit moved back to Scotland again from where it operated along the Norwegian coast, frequently escorting Hampden torpedo-bombers and other raiders. During these operations several Luftwaffe bombers and flying boats were to be encountered during the summer, and a number were shot down.

During September 1943 404 Squadron became a part of the Tain Anti-Shipping Wing, and toward the end of the year converted to Beaufighter Xs, modified to carry rocket projectiles beneath the wings. The Hampdens of 415 Squadron continued to operate over the North Sea, though now mainly by night. Even under cover of darkness losses continued to be heavy, but on 2 August the squadron

managed to damage a U-Boat, which was finished off by a Liberator. In September came a complete change of equipment when the Hampdens were replaced by Leigh Light-equipped Wellington XIIIs, and Fairey Albacores, which were to co-operate in attacking E-Boat surface raiders by night. On 20 January 1944 in one such attack a German destroyer was hit and set on fire by two Albacores, one of which failed to return.

Soon after the departure of 413 Squadron, 422 Squadron had been formed in Northern Ireland with Saro Lerwick flying boats. These proved unsatisfactory, and Catalinas were received instead. Initially the squadron was employed to fly spart parts for Hurricanes to the Soviet Union, the aircraft undertaking some limited patroling over Russian ports while there. In September 1942 these flights ceased and instead the crews ferried Catalinas across the Atlantic until November, when re-equipment with four-engined Short Sunderland IIIs took place. Early in 1943 some escorts were flown to convoys sailing to West Africa, but it was February of that year before the first real operational anti-submarine sorties were flown. The first attack on a U-Boat was recorded on 17 October 1943, but Flt Lt P T Sargent, the pilot responsible, was shot down by return fire from his target.

At the same time as 422, another new flying boat unit has also been formed – 423 Squadron, which was equipped from the start with

Sunderlands, beginning operations in August 1942. Initially the unit was short of aircraft, but by March 1943 it was at full strength, and during that month two attacks were made on U-Boats, Flt Lt Howell and his crew attacking two on 20 March and seeing debris rise to the surface in one case. Success followed rapidly, with one U-Boat attacked by Flt Lt Bradley on 5 April blowing up, while the destruction of another was shared with two destroyers. On 4 August Flg Off A A Bishop attacked U.489, and while his Sunderland was shot down, the submarine was abandoned and blew up as a result of the attack. During the latter part of the year the unit's aircraft frequently flew long-range sorties down to Gibraltar, patroling over Biscay along the way, but two aircraft were lost on these operations.

In 1944 all but one of the RCAF Coastal squadrons were deeply involved in anti-submarine work, joined by the Cansos of 162 Squadron from the home-based air force when this unit was loaned to the RAF in January of that year. Based at Wick in North Scotland, the unit was to sink four U-Boats during its time with the Command, and share a fifth. The most notable occasion was on 24 June 1944 when Flt Lt D E Hornell and his crew sank U.1225. The Canso was badly hit and ditched, but the crew survived although the badly-wounded Hornell, whose skill had saved his companions, died after the rescue. He was awarded the first RCAF Victoria Cross of the war.

Above: Saro Lerwick L7260, an example of the unsuccessful type which first and briefly equipped 422 Squadron. It is seen at Lough Erne, Northern Ireland, in August 1942.
Below: Short Sunderland III flyingboat of 422 Squadron. This aircraft, EK591 'U', gained the only confirmed sinking of a submarine for the squadron, Wt Off W F Norton being the captain of the successful crew on this occasion.

On 10 March 1944 U.625 was abandoned and sank after an attack by Wt Off Martin of 422 Squadron, this unit flying many patrols over the Western Approaches during the year, and also maintaining detachment of Sunderlands in the Shetland Islands. 423 Squadron was also very active, making eight attacks on U-Boats during 1944 for the loss of only one aircraft. Among the older squadrons, 407 and 415 were similarly employed until May, when the latter unit ceased Coastal operations and was transferred to Bomber Command. 407 Squadron, after a period based in Northern Ireland, joined 162 Squadron at Wick in August, but November saw a move to the west of England, following which it was involved in operations against midget submarines operating in the English Channel and off the Dutch coast.

Meanwhile 404 Squadron had moved to Cornwall in May for operations in support of the Normandy Invasion. On D-Day, 6 June, three German destroyers were attacked, at least two of which were damaged, while on the 9th one was caused to beach itself following attacks. In July, the invasion forces well-established ashore, the squadron moved to North Coates for operations off the Dutch coast until much of this fell into Allied hands during the fall. A move to join the Banff Wing for operations against Norwegian coastal targets followed in September, and from here some considerable success was achieved. During an operation against destroyers and minesweepers on 9 February 1945 six Beaufighters were lost, however, the unit's worst casualties of the war.

The next year saw a sharp increase in anti-submarine operations as the Germans introduced new techniques and vessels in a last effort to regain their earlier success, and all four remaining RCAF patrol units were heavily involved, 422 Squadron making four depth charge attacks in three days during March. The last such attack was made by 423 Squadron as late as 4 May, but by then the war was all but over. Like 162 Squadron, 407 had achieved four definite sinkings by the end of the war, and had also damaged at least three more U-Boats, but in its various operations this unit had suffered the heaviest casualties, total losses for the war amounting to 42 Hudsons and Wellingtons.

During April 404 Squadron had exchanged its Beaufighters for Mosquito VIs, but only a few sorties were made before the war ended, and on 25 May the unit was disbanded, while during the month 162 Squadron returned to Canada. 407 Squadron was also disbanded at the start of June, but 422 and 423 Squadrons were both transferred to Transport Command. Their crews moved to Bassingbourn where they were re-equipped with Liberator C.VI and VIII aircraft with which they were to give support to 'Tiger Force' in the Pacific. The sudden ending of the war with Japan in mid-August prevented any operations being undertaken, and on 3 September 1945 both units were also disbanded.

Day Fighters – 2nd Tactical Air Force

The formation of 2nd TAF in November 1943 divided the fighters and fighter-bombers allocated into two Groups, one to support British Second Army and one to support Canadian First Army. Ironically all the RCAF units were allocated to No 83 Group, tasked with the former duty. However, as the Canadians were to advance up the European coast while the British Army went up through central Belgium and Holland, it was the latter area which was to be the focus of the bulk of air combat operations.

All RCAF Spitfire units with the exception of 402 Squadron were initially allocated to 2nd TAF, forming wings at 126 Airfield at Biggin Hill where 401, 411 and 412 Squadrons were led by Wg Cdr McNair, and 127 Airfield at Kenley, where 403 and 421 under the leadership of Wg Cdr Hugh Godefroy would soon be joined by 416 Squadron. Throughout the remaining weeks of 1943 and the opening months of 1944 the Wings were heavily involved in escorting US and RAF medium bombers over the Continent to attack German airfields, transport targets, coastal defenses, and the sites being constructed to launch V-1 flying bombs at England – the latter codenamed 'Noballs'.

In February 1944 144 Airfield was formed with three of the new squadrons from Canada – 441, 442 and 443 – all equipped with Spitfire IXs. Wg Cdr 'Johnny' Johnson returned to command this Wing, while each of the commanding officers was a highly experienced pilot; 441 Squadron was led by Sqn Ldr George Hill who had served in Tunisia and Sicily; 442 Squadron by Battle of Britain veteran Sqn Ldr Blair Russel, and 443 Squadron by No 2 Malta ace, Sqn Ldr Wally McLeod. Indeed during this period large numbers of very experienced RCAF pilots from the Mediterranean theater, and others who had served in the UK-based units, returned for second or third tours, the three Wings reading like a 'Who's Who' of Canadian fighter notables. Wg Cdr George Keefer took over 126 Airfield from 'Buck' McNair during April, and soon afterward the Airfields were officially renamed Wings, moving to the bases from which the invasion would be supported, where pilots began living under canvas. 126 and 127 Wings moved to Tangmere and 144 Wing to Ford. Indeed only one of No 83 Group's fighter Wings was not an RCAF formation.

In the period from November 1943 to the start of June 1944 most squadrons had seen a certain amount of combat, 56 victories being claimed of which 14 were credited to 401 Squadron, all the other units except 442 Squadron claiming at least four. From the moment that the invasion began on 6 June, however, all three wings were heavily engaged, most squadrons achieving considerable success. Patrols over the beachhead and the invasion fleet were interspersed with sweeps inland, and escorts to bomber formations, including RAF Bomber Command 'heavies' bombing in direct support of the armies. A few German bombers were encountered in the opening

Below: One of the RCAF's greatest fighter pilots and leaders, Wg Cdr R W 'Buck' McNair DSO, DFC★★, who commanded 126 Wing at Biggin Hill during the early months of 1944. A veteran of Malta, McNair was credited with 16 victories.

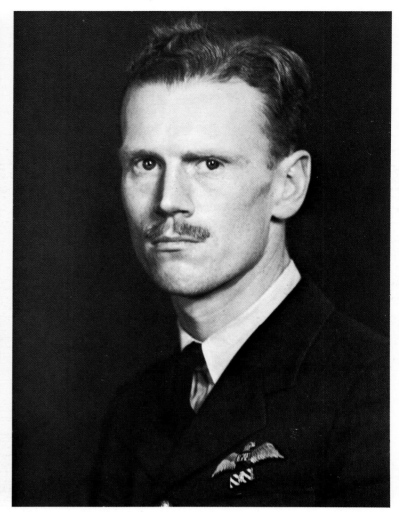

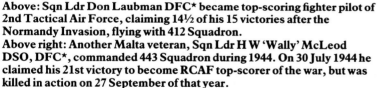

Above: Sqn Ldr Don Laubman DFC★ became top-scoring fighter pilot of 2nd Tactical Air Force, claiming 14½ of his 15 victories after the Normandy Invasion, flying with 412 Squadron.
Above right: Another Malta veteran, Sqn Ldr H W 'Wally' McLeod DSO, DFC★, commanded 443 Squadron during 1944. On 30 July 1944 he claimed his 21st victory to become RCAF top-scorer of the war, but was killed in action on 27 September of that year.

days, and a dozen Ju 88s and Do 217s were claimed, but most fighting was with the Bf 109s and Fw 190s of the Jagdflieger.

Losses generally were remarkably light considering the number and ferocity of the engagements which occurred over the battle zone during June and July. A sad loss occurred on 13 June, however, when Wg Cdr Chadburn and another pilot collided; both died. R A Buckham was promoted from command of 403 Squadron to replace him. 144 Wing became the first to move to French soil on 15 June, followed next day by 127 Wing, and by 126 Wing on 18th. George Keefer's tour ended early in July by which time he had added four more victories to raise his score to nine, and he was replaced at the head of 126 Wing by Blair Russel from 442 Squadron. On 13 July to everyone's surprise, 144 Wing, which had achieved the best results since D-Day, was disbanded. 441, 442 and 443 Squadrons were transferred to 125 (RAF), 126 and 127 Wings respectively, 'Johnny' Johnson going to take over the latter from Buckham.

Following the slogging battles around Caen, and the slaughter of the German Seventh Army at Falaise, the Allied breakout began during late August and by the end of the month the Germans had retreated out of most of France and were being pursued through Belgium into Holland and Germany. By the end of August, in less than three months, the nine Canadian squadrons had claimed between them some 262 victories for relatively minimal combat losses. Again 401 Squadron was the most successful unit with 47½, followed by 441 Squadron with 35. Among the pilots 'Johnny' Johnson had been the most successful once more with nine personal victories, followed by 401 Squadron's commander, Hugh Trainor, with 8½, and by two other 'stars' of this unit, G W Johnson with

seven and W T 'Grissle' Klersy with six; 443 Squadron's Wally McLeod also had six.

The general German withdrawal brought a reduction in contact with the enemy through much of late August and early September, but the Allied airborne landings in Holland later in the latter month brought the Luftwaffe out again. This was particularly so around Nijmegen where repeated attacks were made in an attempt to destroy the bridge there, which had been captured by the US paratroops. Fighting here brought 99 victories in six days, 25-30 September, for the Canadians, 30 of them for 412 Squadron alone. This unit claimed nine on the 26th and 15 on the 27th – including four by Flt Lt Don Laubman. On this latter date 411 Squadron claimed eight, while on the 29th 401 Squadron claimed nine. Casualties during this heavy fighting were more severe than they had been over Normandy, 17 Spitfires being lost, including Sqn Ldr Wally McLeod, who was shot down and killed on 27 September. With his personal score at 21 he was top-scoring RCAF pilot of the war.

At the end of September the squadrons of 125 Wing exchanged their Spitfire IXEs for 126 Wing's older Mark IXBs, all four units then withdrawing to England, 441 Squadron included. To replace them five squadrons of Spitfire XIVs flew out from the UK to join 125 Wing, including 402 Squadron which was now flying these powerful Griffon-engined machines. Wing Leader was RCAF pilot George Keefer, beginning his third tour; he would add four further victories with this RAF Wing to raise his total to 13 by the end of the war.

Meanwhile operations over Nijmegen continued in early October, the importance of the target bringing out some of the new Messerschmitt Me 262 jet fighter-bombers – the first to be met by 2nd TAF. The first victory over one of these high-performance aircraft to be claimed by the Tactical Air Force, was achieved on 5 October by five pilots of 401 Squadron led by Malta veteran Sqn Ldr R I A Smith; Rod Smith had claimed seven other victories since July to raise his total to 13⅕. Next day the Spitfire XIVs of 402 Squadron were in

Above: Sqn Ldr R I A Smith DFC★ led four other 401 Squadron pilots to shoot down the first Me 262 jet fighter to be credited to 2nd TAF aircraft on 5 October 1944. Another who had gained his early victories over Malta, Rod Smith would end the war with a personal total of 13 and the shared jet.

action over the area for the first time, three Bf 109s and an Fw 190 being claimed without loss.

With reduced Luftwaffe opposition to be found after the Nijmegen interlude, squadrons began returning to the UK in rotation to attend armament practise camps to practise dive-bombing, and soon both wings were regularly carrying 1000 pound bomb loads – a 500 pound bomb beneath the fuselage and a 250 pound beneath each wing – to augment the strafing which was becoming a frequent feature of their offensive reconnaissance sweeps. Combats were of a desultory nature during the fall, but on 24 October Flt Lt Laubman shot down two Fw 190s to raise his personal score to 15 – 14½ of them since D-Day, making him 2nd TAF top-scorer of the war.

Very bad weather as winter drew in reduced flying considerably. In conditions of fog and snow the German Ardennes offensive was launched in mid-December, but at first there was little the Allied air forces could do. The weather cleared completely on Christmas Eve, and over the next week the Luftwaffe was met in great force. Again 126 and 127 Wings were much involved. Some 28 victories were claimed before the turn of the year, 13 of these by 411 Squadron. In this unit a new flight commander of great flying skill but no previous combat experience, Flt Lt R J Audet, claimed three Fw 190s and two Bf 109s shot down in a single combat on 29 December – the only Spitfire pilot ever to gain five victories during a single sortie. Within a month Dick Audet would have raised his total to 10½, including one of the new Me 262 jets, but he was to be killed during the last week of the war, a victim of the deadly German light Flak. Me 262s formed two more of the RCAF victories during the Ardennes operations, 403 and 411 Squadrons each claiming one on Christmas Day.

The other RCAF fighter unit, 402 Squadron, claimed a single victory on this date, but on the 29th the squadron was transferred from 125 to 126 Wing, to fly with the other Canadian units. On 1 January 1945 came the great Luftwaffe New Year's Day attack on the Allied airfields, Operation 'Bödenplatte'. The attack on 126 Wing's airfield at Heesch found most squadrons already airborne, or taking off, and failed to catch any aircraft on the ground. The Wing enjoyed its greatest single success to date, claiming 24 and three probables for the loss of one Spitfire shot down and one crash-landed. At Evere 127 Wing was less fortunate; one aircraft was shot

Above: Only Spitfire pilot ever to claim five victories in a single sortie was ex-instructor Flt Lt R J 'Dick' Audet DFC★. The 411 Squadron flight commander would raise his tally to 10½ after his noteable success of 29 December 1944, before being shot down and killed by Flak while attacking a train on 3 March 1945.

Below: A Spitfire XIV of 402 Squadron. In this aircraft, RN119 'J', Flg Off C B McConnell shot down a Ju 88 on 19 April 1945, flying from Wunstorf airfield, Germany.

down as it took off and three more were strafed as they taxied. At the end of the attack 11 Spitfires had been detroyed on the ground and 12 more damaged; only 403 Squadron was in the air, claiming six victories.

Losses were quickly made good, and during the month 443 Squadron exchanged its Spitfire IXs for Mark XVIs. These were virtually identical aircraft, but powered by US Packard-built Merlin engines. Appearing in increasing quantities, these aircraft were soon to re-equip the whole of 127 Wing. A high point in January for 126 Wing occurred on the 23rd when jets were seen operating from an airstrip north of Osnabruck. 401 Squadron attacked, and three were claimed shot down in the circuit, while later in the day another was claimed over the same area by 411 Squadron.

As the weather improved, offensive operations increased again on the ground and in the air, and during March more action was seen. On the 12th 401 Squadron again shot down an Me 262 – its fifth jet – while next day one fell to 402 Squadron to raise the Canadians' 'bag' of jets to nine. Furing February 442 Squadron had left 126 Wing and withdrawn to England to rejoin No 11 Group, but other units continued to operate in Europe until the end of the war. Before leaving, 442 Squadron had enjoyed some good fortune on two occasions during February. On the 8th five night ground attack Ju 87s were caught at dawn and all were shot down, while on the 25th seven Bf 109s were claimed without loss from a large formation encountered over Rheine. During these later months of the war much emphasis was given to ground attack, and in consequence losses to ground fire rose quite sharply. Don Laubman had been promoted to command the Spitfire XIV-equipped 402 Squadron in April, but on the 14th he was shot down by Flak and became a prisoner. 126 Wing moved onto German soil during this month as the armies advanced deep into that country. The final days of the war saw a resurgence of activity as Luftwaffe units withdrawing before the Russian forces came within reach of 2nd TAF units, and as many Germans attempted to fly out to Scandinavia. On 20 April alone 401 Squadron claimed 18 victories, three and one shared by Sqn Ldr Bill Klersy to bring his score to 14½, second only to Laubman. Eleven victories were claimed by 412 Squadron during this period, and ten by 403 Squadron, while the other five units claimed a further 20. The last claim was made on 4 May when Flg Off O'Brien of 411 Squadron shot down an He 111 bomber; 28 aircraft were also claimed destroyed on the ground, or moored on the water (floatplanes). On 6 May 125 Wing released a number of Spitfire XIVs to re-equip 401 Squadron, but it was too late – the European war was over.

The RCAF contribution to the 2nd TAF fighter force had been tremendous; 126 Wing was that air force's top-scorer with 361 air and 12 ground victories with 156 losses; within the wing, 401 Squadron was top-scoring 2nd TAF fighter unit with 112 air and 15 ground victories. 127 Wing came fourth on the list of wing scores, with 184:8:103. Among individual fighter pilots the two top scorers, Laubman and Klersy, were Canadians, while 'Johnny' Johnson with 13 victories while with 2nd TAF was third highest-scorer, and had gained all his victories flying with the Canadians. Other high scorers included John MacKay of 401 Squadron with 11⅕ and Dick Audet of 411 Squadron with 10½; three more RCAF pilots had claimed nine victories since November 1943, and four others eight.

All units remained in Germany after the conclusion of hostilities, but disbandments soon began. First to go was 403 Squadron in June, followed next month by 401, 402 and 421 Squadrons. 411, 412, 416 and 443 Squadrons continued until March 1946, but all four were stood down during that month.

With Fighter Command, 1944-45

Before its move to Belgium in September 1944, 402 Squadron had undertaken dive-bombing operations, patrols and bomber escorts until August, when conversion from Spitfire IXs to Mark XIVs brought an involvement in the last weeks of operations against the V-1s. These latter sorties were undertaken from Hawkinge, coupled with some sweeps over the Dutch coast. 402 Squadron was replaced at the end of September by 441 Squadron on its return from Europe, this unit undertaking a number of escort missions to Bomber Command daylight raids until December.

In February 1945 442 Squadron arrived back from Europe without aircraft, and was posted to Hunsdon to re-equip with Mustang IVs (P-51Ds) and became a part of one of the new RAF Mustang Wing to undertake escorts to the 'heavies' over Germany. Operating with 611 Squadron, RAF, the unit was to claim three air and six ground victories during the last days of the war on these duties. 441 Squadron had returned to Hawkinge during the month to resume escorts, but then moved to Digby to convert to Mustangs, the war ending before any operations could be flown. Both units were disbanded at the start of August 1945.

Below: Consolidated Catalina IB, W8438 of 413 Squadron, based in the Shetland Islands before its departure for the Indian Ocean late in 1941.

The Fighter-Bombers

Of the six ex-home based RCAF fighter units which arrived in the United Kingdom late in 1943, three – 438, 439 and 440 Squadrons – were destined to become fighter-bomber units, forming 143 Airfield at Hurn in early 1944. Prior to this, they had worked up with Hurricane IVs in the Midlands, but had re-equipped with Typhoon IBs during February. While many RAF Typhoon units were fitted to fire rocket projectiles from beneath the wings, the Canadian units were to specialize in bombing, each aircraft carrying a pair of 500lb bombs as normal offensive load. First operations were flown on 20 March by 438 Squadron, and by the end of the month the whole wing was operational, led by Wg Cdr R T P Davidson, a notable Canadian fighter pilot who had flown in the Middle East and from Ceylon, including German, Italian and Japanese aircraft among his victories.

The first loss was suffered on 10 April when a 439 Squadron aircraft failed to return, but on 24th 438 Squadron became the first Typhoon unit to drop 1000lb bombs against a 'Noball' target. On 8 May Davidson's aircraft suffered an engine failure while he was leading 438 Squadron to dive-bomb marshalling yards, and he was obliged to force-land in France; his place at the head of the wing was taken by M T Judd, DFC, another ex-Middle East ace.

Like other RCAF units, 143 Wing served with No 83 Group of 2nd TAF, and was extremely active following the start of the invasion in June 1944, moving to bases in Normandy around the middle of the month. Losses of Typhoons, by the very nature of their duties, were heavy. Most were victims of light Flak and other ground fire, although quite a number suffered from crashes occasioned by malfunctioning of their powerful, but temperamental, Sabre engines at low altitude, while not a few flew into obstructions while engaged in their attacks. General interdiction and close support targets included supply columns, artillery positions and bunkers, command posts and headquarters, bridges and rail junctions. During the invasion period 438 and 439 Squadrons escaped relatively lightly, but 440 Squadron lost eight aircraft during June alone. Over Falaise in August the wing was particularly active, and during the general German retreat that followed. October 1944 found the wing established at Eindhoven in Holland, and here Wg Cdr Judd was replaced by F G Grant, previously commander of 438 Squadron.

Above: Sqn Ldr John MacKay DFC★ gained 11 and one shared victories with 401 Squadron during 1944/5, adding a MiG 15 over Korea when on attachment to the USAF in 1953. He is seen here with a Canadair Sabre when commanding 416 Squadron in the early fifties.

The wing was heavily involved in the operations over the Ardennes during late 1944, and here became engaged in an increased amount of aerial combat as the Luftwaffe attempted to interfere with the close support squadrons. On Christmas Eve 438 Squadron lost two Typhoons during a strafe, while 400 lost a third. Then while covering a further operation two more of the latter unit's aircraft were shot down by an Fw 190, which itself was shot down by an RAF Tempest. Bombing in the St Vith area on the 27th 440 Squadron aircraft engaged three Bf 109s, one of which was shot down, while two days later Flg Off R H Laurence of 439 Squadron claimed two Fw 190s – one of them one of the powerful long-nosed 'D' models.

The wing was one of the most hard-hit during the 1 January 1945 Luftwaffe attack, 438 and 440 Squadrons being about to take off when the German fighters appeared. One Typhoon was shot down as it took off and a second was hit as it was on its take-off run, the pilot being mortally wounded. Several others were hit, 12 being destroyed in all. Four of 439 Squadron's aircraft were already in the air on a weather reconnaissance, and these engaged 15 Fw 190s, Flg Off Laurence and Flg Off A H Fraser claiming two each, though one of the other Typhoons was shot down.

The wing was back up to strength within two days, and it was 439 Squadron which gained more success in the air on 14 February when two Me 262 jets were seen and bounced, both being shot down. Close support operations increased again during the spring with the Anglo-Canadian offensives which began during February and March, culminating in the Rhine crossing late in the latter month. The last encounter with the Luftwaffe came on 3 April when 438 Squadron was bounced by a dozen or so Bf 109s, two top-cover Typhoons being shot down. However, of over 100 Typhoons lost by the wing during the course of operations, no more than eight are known to have fallen to enemy fighters – and one to an Allied P-47!

During April the wing moved to B150 airfield on German soil, and from here the units were sent in rotation to the UK for armament practice camp. Indeed 440 Squadron was still so engaged when the war came to an end. The last two weeks of the war saw considerable action over the Baltic in search of shipping and aircraft trying to reach Denmark and Norway. Here on 24 April 439 Squadron strafed and destroyed a six-engined Bv 222 flying boat on the water, while at the start of May two more German aircraft were shot down by pilots of this unit to raise its tally to 11 in the air and one on the water; the two other units ended the war with a single victory each. However, the measure of 143 Wing's success had been the large number of ground targets which it had destroyed as its main function. In achieving these results 439 Squadron had suffered the heaviest casualties, losing 38 aircraft, while 440 lost 36 and 438 lost 27; all but five of this total went down after the invasion had begun.

Transport Command

Several Bomber and Coastal Command units were transferred to Transport Command after the close of hostilities in Europe, while two transport squadrons were formed overseas. A single unit of this type saw service from the United Kingdom during the war years; this was 437 Squadron, the last new RCAF unit to be formed outside Canada during the war, which came into being early in September 1944, equipped with Douglas Dakotas. Within days of its formation 14 of the unit's aircraft were towing gliders to Arnhem for the airborne landings there on 17 September, more being pulled across next day. Resupply flights to the area were made on 21st and 23rd, but in the face of stiff resistance from Flak and fighters, Transport Command losses were heavy and four of the Dakotas which did not return were 437 Squadron aircraft.

Following these initial operations, the squadron settled down to a

Below: Dakota FD946 of 436 Squadron over Burma. Note that the overpainted bars of a USAAF insignia can be seen behind the fuselage roundel, indicating the aircraft's origin.
Above right: Although not a member of the RCAF until late in the war, Canadian Flt Lt George 'Screwball' Beurling DSO, DFC, DFM★, was the nation's highest-scoring fighter pilot of the war with 31⅓ personal victories, all but five claimed over Malta, where he was the RAF's top-scorer. He served with 412 Squadron late in 1943.

more gentle round of supply shuttle missions to the armies in Europe. A number of Ansons were added to strength during November. A return to more active duties occurred in March 1945 when involvement in Operation 'Varsity', the airborne crossing of the Rhine, saw the Dakotas towing 24 Horsa gliders into the drop zone. On conclusion of hostilities the unit was involved in bringing liberated prisoners of war to England, and repatriating Canadian troops from Canadian First Army to the UK for shipment home. During July 1945 a detachment was maintained at Oslo in Norway, and in October one was set up in Berlin. The following month saw a move to Odiham, with a small detachment at Evere in Belgium, while in 1946 flights were conducted increasingly from the old Imperial Airways airfield at Croydon. In mid-June of that year the squadron was disbanded.

Air Observation Post

Three squadrons equipped with Auster light aircraft were formed late in 1944 for operations with the Canadian First Army, most personnel being members of the army. 664 and 665 Squadrons began operations during 1945, but the third unit, 666 Squadron, was not operational before the war ended.

The RCAF in Other Theaters

As was the case in Western Europe, the contribution of the RCAF in terms of aircrew personnel to the operations of the RAF was very considerable in those areas in which the latter was involved. Numbers of Canadians in the RAF were serving in the Middle East from the outbreak of the war there in June 1940, and these were soon joined by considerable numbers of RCAF personnel to serve both in the Western Deserts of Egypt and Libya, and in defense of the island of Malta. Indeed some of the most notable of the Canadians with the RAF were to make their names here, such as Wg Cdr Vernon Woodward, who was credited with 19 and two shared victories flying in the Desert and Greece with 33 Squadron, RAF, in 1941-41, and the greatest Canadian fighter ace of the war, Flt Lt George 'Screwball' Beurling, who claimed 26⅓ of his 31⅓ victories while flying from Malta during 1942. Second only to Beurling on Malta

was the RCAF pilot who would become that air force's top-scorer of the war, Wally McLeod (Beurling was the top-scoring Canadian 'per se'). Like McLeod, many other leading RCAF fighter pilots who later served with distinction in the Canadian units in Western Europe gained their baptism of fire in the Middle East. Typical of these were WG Cdr J F 'Stocky' Edwards, who claimed 16½ victories flying Kittyhawks and Spitfires over North Africa and Italy, George Hill who led an RAF Spitfire squadron in Tunisia and over Sicily, being credited here with ten and six shared victories, and Irving Kennedy who claimed six and four shared over Sicily and Italy during 1943. George Keefer, later a successful Wing Leader in 2nd TAF, claimed five in the Desert in 1942, flying the elderly Hurricane, while night fighter 'Moose' Fumerton operated over Egypt and Malta in his 89 Squadron Beaufighter, claiming 11 air and one ground victory during the same period. On Malta the success of Beurling and McLeod was mirrored by other Canadians; J W 'Willie the Kid' Williams was credited with ten victories, R W 'Buck' McNair with eight, while R I A Smith claimed six and his brother got another four before his death in action. A member of the RCAF who also shone on Malta was American Claude Weaver III, who gained 11½ of his total on the island. Indeed during the early months of the war in Africa, the RAF in Egypt was commanded by that old World War I 'warhorse', AVM Raymond Collishaw.

In the Far East, too, members of the RCAF were among early reinforcements sent from England to Singapore, the East Indies and Burma. Notable among these were H H 'Snooks' Everard, who shot down one Japanese fighter during the retreat from Burma, R T P Davidson, who claimed four victories against German and Italian aircraft over Greece and added two Japanese to his score in defense of Ceylon; later in the war R W R Day arrived from the UK after service with RCAF units there, becoming the first Canadian pilot to claim victories over five Japanese aircraft while commanding 67 Squadron, RAF. Although not a member of the RCAF, another Canadian – D J Sheppard – was also to claim five victories against the Japanese while flying Corsair fighters from a Royal Navy aircraft carrier as a member of the RCNVR. Another member of this force became only the second Commonwealth fighter pilot to be awarded a Victoria Cross in World War II. This was Lt Robert Hampton Gray who received a posthumous award for a determined bombing attack on a Japanese frigate during the last days of the war.

While RCAF involvement in RAF units was maintained at such a high level, the number of Canadian squadrons operating outside Western Europe was extremely limited, although the very variety of those involved provides a good illustration of the wide range of duties and activities involved. The first such involvement did not arise until March 1942, in which month two RCAF squadrons in the UK were ordered to cease operations and proceed overseas. The first of these was 413 Squadron, a Catalina flying boat unit, recently formed within Coastal Command, which despatched its first batch of aircraft forthwith, destination Ceylon in the Indian Ocean. Here Japanese naval action was feared, following the recent fall of the Indies and of Rangoon, capital of Burma. The first Catalinas reached Koggala harbor on 2 April, and were at once readied to join the resident flying boats of 205 Squadron, RAF, in the search for the enemy fleet.

First sighting was made by Sqn Ldr L J Birchall of 413 Squadron on 4 April, when he found Admiral Nagumo's Carrier Striking Force 350 miles to the southeast at 1600 hours and radioed a warning. The flying boat was then intercepted and shot down by Zero fighters from the carriers. Next day Colombo suffered a severe and damaging raid, but the carriers then disappeared again. Searching continued, and the vessels were again found by a 413 Squadron aircraft early on the 9th. Flt Lt Rae Thomas, DFC, a South African, and one of the unit's most experienced pilots, also managed to give a warning, but his aircraft then also fell victim to the fighters, a heavy raid on Trincomalee in the north of the island following later in the morning. After these attacks the carriers withdrew, never to return to the Indian Ocean.

Following the excitements and losses of the April operations, the rest of the war was to prove somewhat of an anticlimax for 413. No further attacks developed, and its duties as an anti-submarine patrol and convoy escort squadron were rarely enlivened by action of any sort. Throughout the next two and a half years submarines were sighted on several occasions, and attacks were made. While at least two were believed damaged, no definite sinking could ever be claimed. A number of detachments were undertaken by elements of the unit to Aden, St Lucia, Durban, Tulear and the Seychelles Islands, but in December 1944 the unit was stood down from operations and in January 1945 flew back to the United Kingdom, where it was disbanded a month later.

The other unit to leave the UK in March 1942 was one of the new Spitfire squadrons – 417. Their aircraft were left behind, the long journey to Egypt – the destination of the squadron – being undertaken by sea via the Cape of Good Hope and the Suez Canal. At last the destination was reached in June, but there followed a long period on base defense duties, initially flying Hurricanes, with which a single Ju 88 was shot down, and then Spitfires. Although the unit began moving up to join 244 Wing, RAF, at the front early in 1943, it was retained for some time for the defense of Tripoli, where a second victory was gained over an He 111 torpedo-bomber.

At last, in April 1943 the unit moved up to begin operations as part

Previous pages: Catalina I W8406 coded AX-D serving with the Ceylon-based 413 Squadron.

of the wing in Tunisia, but on its second day over the front its inexperience resulted in it suffering a severe 'bounce' by 20 Bf 109s, which shot down four of the Spitfires and damaged a fifth without loss. Later in the month two Axis fighters were shot down while the squadron was involved in escorting Kittyhawks over the Cap Bon area, but when hostilities in Africa ceased early in May, the wing settled down to rest and prepare for the forthcoming invasion of Sicily. Early in July 417 Squadron was taken over by one of the great RAF Canadian fighter pilots, Sqn Ldr Stan Turner, DFC, who had flown during 1940 in 242 Squadron. Under Turner's guidance the unit moved to Malta, making its first patrol over Sicily on 10 July – the day of the landings. On the 18th a move was made to Cassibile on Sicilian soil, and then steadily across the island to Lentini, on the north coast. Here in August came re-equipment with the splendid new Spitfire VIII air superiority fighter, with which the unit flew sweeps, scrambles and patrols during the invasion of southern Italy by the Eighth Army. Moves to the mainland, to Grottaglie, Gioia delle Colle, and then Foggia, continued through September.

While 417 Squadron had been so involved, further RCAF units had arrived in the area, albeit on a temporary basis only. As it had become clear that the end was close in Tunisia, three squadrons of Wellington X bombers from No 6 (RCAF) Group of Bomber Command were readied for the move to North Africa to assist in the forthcoming invasions of southern Europe. Consequently during April 1943 420, 424 and 425 Squadrons flew to Beaufarik in Algeria, subsequently taking up base at Kairouan in Tunisia. From here the Wellingtons were soon in action, raiding targets in Sicily and southern Italy by night. While so engaged, they formed 351 Wing as part of No 205 Group, RAF, in the Allied North-West African Strategic Air Force.

While no longer faced by the mighty Flak barrage of the Ruhr or the marauding night fighters of the Luftwaffe Reichsverteidigung (Home Defense), the Canadian bomber crews swiftly discovered that the night skies over southern Europe were no picnic. During a raid on Sicilian targets during the night of 26/27 June, Plt Off Taschereau's 425 Squadron crew spotted a Ju 88 night fighter, which attacked them, damaging the Wellington and badly wounding the wireless operator. The rear gunner returned fire, seeing hits and believing that he had sent the interceptor down in flames into the sea. However, a second of the unit's bombers failed to return from the night's mission – the first of 18 Wellingtons to be lost before operations ceased early in October. 420 and 424 Squadrons were to bear the bulk of the casualties, losing at least seven aircraft each, and two bombers would be lost in a night on four occasions as targets such as Messina port, San Giovanni marshalling yards and Naples were attacked. The three squadrons continued to operate throughout the Sicilian landings, and those in southern Italy, only returning to their British bases in October, when the whole of southern Italy was finally in Allied hands, and the rest of No 205 Group began moving forward to bases in Italy.

Even as the bomber crews prepared to leave, 417 Squadron gained its first victory over Italy, one of 12 Fw 190 Jabos (fighter-bombers) being shot down into the sea off Vasto by Flt Lt A U Houle, DFC, another of the experienced Canadian pilots who had served with the RAF in North Africa, and was now a flight commander. During the last two months of the year the squadron was involved with patrols and escorts over the battle taking place at the Sangro River, and here during late November/early December the Luftwaffe again attempted to intervene, five victories being claimed at this time to double the unit's 'bag' to date; two of these fell to Houle.

The rest of December proved uneventful and the squadron even engaged in some strafing, also undertaking its first operation over Yugoslavia on 8 January 1944. On New Year's Day the whole camp – based on the sand dunes by the sea – had been almost washed away in a violent storm which led to widespread flooding. On 16 January the 'A' Party moved across Italy to Marcianise, near Naples, from where high cover patrols were to be flown over the Anzio area, where Allied landings were made late in the month. Now the squadron enjoyed its greatest success, intercepting formations of Fw 190 Jabos and their Messerschmitt escorts, and by the end of February nine victories had been claimed for the loss of only two Spitfires. Four of

Much strafing was undertaken, and during June the squadron began carrying 500lb bombs, but on 16th June Flak took its toll of the strafers, Bruce Ingalls being shot down and killed with his personal score at seven. By August the unit was again fully equipped with Mark VIIIs, and was engaged in some escorts to medium bombers, but nothing was seen in opposition. Losses to Flak totalled four in July, but only two throughout August and September. Not until December were opposing aircraft seen, but two engagements during that month and January 1945 with reluctant Bf 109 pilots of the Italian Fascist RSI, brought no conclusive results. The final offensive of 1945 resulted in several more losses to Flak, while in early April the Spitfire VIIIs were finally changed for fighter-bomber Mark IXs. The end of the war in early May found the unit newly moved to Treviso, where it was disbanded.

Meanwhile far away in India, two new RCAF units had been formed during October 1944. 435 and 436 Squadrons were both raised at Gujrat in the Punjab, equipped with Dakota III and IV transports for service on the Burma front. Here air transportation was a vital prerequisite of Allied offensive success, and great efforts were being made to increase RAF strength in this respect before USAAF transport units, which provided the bulk of the force, were withdrawn to China.

While still training, 436 Squadron aided 117 Squadron, RAF, in a move to the forward area during December, but it was 435 which went into action first, moving to Tulihal airfield on 19 December and making its first air drop of supplies to the forward troops next day. These operations were undertaken in support of XXXIII Corps in the Schwebo area, and while five of the squadron's aircraft were in the dropping circuit here on 12 January 1945, a number of Nakajima Ki 43 'Oscar' fighters attacked, shooting down two of the Dakotas and driving the others away. In one aircraft only one man was killed, but in the other only the co-pilot survived.

Three days after this incident 436 Squadron, which had arrived at Kangla, began operating over the same area, but during these early weeks both units were very short of equipment. 435 Squadron, having flown no less than 2325 sorties in January, added 1054 more in February. One loss was suffered on the 12th of this month, but on the 25th, 11 aircraft took part in a special operation supporting an attack on Japanese airfields south of Meiktila. At the start of March flights into Meiktila were made, and here crews were able to see Thunderbolts dive-bombing the front line nearby, while Spitfires, Mustangs and Mosquitos patroled overhead. 436 Squadron moved to Akyab Island on 17 March, and both units were active flying supplies into Meiktila and surrounding airfields. Both at this time were supplemented with a number of Beech C-45 Expeditor light transports.

Late in April wireless operators from both units received special training as 'Jumpmasters' for Operation 'Dracula', the forthcoming airborne assault on Elephant Point, Rangoon. This operation took place on 1 May, but the Canadian Dakotas did not take part, the Jumpmasters from the two squadrons carrying out their tasks aboard US troop carriers of the 1st and 2nd Air Commando Groups. The aircraft were soon flying down to the area, however, carrying the second lift of reinforcement troops.

After this 435 Squadron was busy flying into Meiktila, Myingyan and Sinthe, while 436 Squadron was much involved supplying troops operating from the newly captured Ramree Island. This unit had one of the more notable RCAF two-tour expired fighter pilots, Flt Lt A F 'Butch' Aikman, DFC and Bar, flying with it as the only way he could get back on operations again. After the Rangoon sorties, June, July and August were involved mainly in the mopping up of retreating troops. 435 Squadron became involved in carrying rice to starving communities in North Burma.

The war ended in mid-August, and so 435 Squadron began running down in India, and the Dakotas were flown to the United Kingdom where the unit was re-formed. After a short period of casualty evacuation work in South-East Asia, 436 Squadron followed suit, joining 435 at Down Ampney late in September. Here both units became involved in general European transport work until 435 Squadron was disbanded in April 1946; 436 was similarly stood down two months later.

Above: Wg Cdr George Keefer DSO★, DFC★, saw considerable service as a Hurricane pilot in the Western Desert of North Africa with 274 Squadron, RAF, before leading Spitfire Wings with 2nd TAF. He ended the war with a personal score of 13.

the victories were credited to Bert Houle, now commanding officer, while three and two probables went to the ex-Burma pilot, 'Snooks' Everard, now a flight commander in 417. At the end of the month Houle, awarded a Bar to his DFC, was rested, and soon after Everard also finished his tour.

March brought seven more victories, two of them by Flt Lt Bruce Ingalls, another experienced pilot who had taken over Everard's flight, as the rest of the squadron moved over to Marcianise. During a big fight on 29 March against 20 fighters, Plt Off J J Doyle, who would later fly for Israel in 1948, shot down a Bf 109 and claimed an Fw 190 probable, although his own aircraft was in flames; he crash-landed safely, although another Spitfire was shot down during this engagement.

During April 1944 'B' Flight re-equipped temporarily with Spitfire IXs due to shortage of Mark VIIIs, the unit moving to Venafro, near the famous Cassino hill, where the long siege was moving to its climax. From here detachments continued to be sent into the Anzio beachhead to operate from the Nettuno airstrip there. Two victories in April were followed by two in May for the loss of a single Spitfire, but these were to be 417's last successes in the air, bringing the total to 29. As Cassino fell and the Allied forces advanced toward Rome, came news of the Normandy landings, followed by the great Russian summer offensive. The result was an almost total withdrawal from Italy of the remaining Luftwaffe units, leaving even the Spitfire VIII squadrons with only ground support activities to engage them.

RCAF Overseas; Order of Battle, April 1945

Bomber Command

No 6 (RCAF) Group

62 (Beaver) Base

408, 426 Squadrons	Linton-on-Ouse	Halifax VII
415 Squadron	East Moor	Halifax III & VII
432 Squadron	East Moor	Halifax III
420 Squadron	Tholthorpe	Lancaster I, X, Halifax III
425 Squadron	Tholthorpe	Halifax III

63 Base

427, 429 Squadrons	Leeming	Lancaster I, III, Halifax III
424 Squadron	Skipton-on-Swale	Lancaster I & III
433 Squadron	Skipton-on-Swale	Lancaster I & III, Halifax III

64 Base

419, 428 Squadrons	Middleton St George	Lancaster X
431, 434 Squadrons	Croft	Lancaster X

No 8 Group (PFF)

405 Squadron	Gransden Lodge	Lancaster I & III

Below: Sqn Ldr R A Kipp DSO, DFC★ was a leading Mosquito pilot.

Fighter Command

No 11 Group

406 Squadron	Manston	Mosquito XXX
442 Squadron	Hunsdon	Mustang IV

No 12 Group

441 Squadron	Digby	Spitfire IXB, Mustang III

Coastal Command

No 15 Group

407 Squadron	Chivenor	Wellington XIV
422 Squadron	Pembroke Dock	Sunderland III
423 Squadron	Castle Archdale (det. at Pembroke Dock)	Sunderland III

No 18 Group

404 Squadron	Banff	Mosquito VI
162 Squadron	Wick	Canso

2nd Tactical Air Force

No 2 Group

136 Wing

418 Squadron	Coxyde, B71	Mosquito VI

No 83 Group

39 (Recce) Wing

400 Squadron	Schneverdingen, B154	Spitfire XI
414, 430 Squadrons	Schneverdingen, B154	Spitfire XIVB

126 Wing

401, 411, 412 Squadrons	Wunstorf, B116	Spitfire IXE
402 Squadron	Wunstorf, B116	Spitfire XIV

127 Wing

403, 416, 421, 443 Squadrons	Schneverdingen, B154	Spitfire XVI

143 Wing

438, 439, 440 Squadrons	Fassberg, B150	Typhoon IB

No 85 Group

147 Wing

410 Squadron	Gilze-Rijen, B77	Mosquito XXX

148 Wing

409 Squadron	Rheine, B108	Mosquito XIII

Transport Command

No 46 Group

437 Squadron	Blakehill Farm	Dakota, Anson

Desert Air Force, Italy

244 Wing

417 Squadron	Bellaria	Spitfire IX

Eastern Air Command, India/Burma 3rd Tactical Air Force

435 Squadron	Tulihal	Dakota, Expeditor

341 Wing

436 Squadron	Mawnubyin	Dakota, Expeditor

Aerial Victory Totals of RCAF Fighter, Night-Fighter, Fighter-Bomber and Fighter-Reconnaissance Squadrons

401/1 Squadron	173½	402 Squadron	49
403 Squadron	119⅔	406 Squadron	47½
412 Squadron	113	443 Squadron	35
418 Squadron	101	417 Squadron	29
421 Squadron	92	414 Squadron	28½
411 Squadron	82	400 Squadron	11
410 Squadron	73½	439 Squadron	11
416 Squadron	67	430 Squadron	2
409 Squadron	60	438 Squadron	1
442 Squadron	54	440 Squadron	1
441 Squadron	50		

Below: Commanding officer of 417 Squadron in Italy was Sqn Ldr A U Houle DFC, a long-serving Middle East front fighter pilot with 11 personal victories.

Top-scoring RCAF Fighter Pilots

Sqn Ldr H W McLeod	21
Wg Cdr R W McNair	17
Wg Cdr J F Edwards	16½
Sqn Ldr D C Laubman	14 & 2 shared
Sqn Ldr W T Klersy	14½
Sqn Ldr R I A Smith	13⅕
Wg Cdr R C Fumerton	13
Wg Cdr G C Keefer	13
Flt Lt J F McElroy	12 & 3 shared*
Flt Lt J MacKay	12⅕**
Flt Lt J H Turnbull	12½
Sqn Ldr G U Hill	10 & 8 shared
Flt Lt R J Audet	10½
Sqn Ldr R A Kipp	10½
Sqn Ldr J D Mitchner	10½
Flt Lt D W Schmidt	10½
Wg Cdr J E Walker	10½
Sqn Ldr A U Houle	10
Plt Off J W Williams	10
Sqn Ldr D C Gordon	9 & 2 shared
Flt Lt I F Kennedy	8 & 4 shared

* Later got 2 or 3 victories flying with Israel in 1948
** Includes 1 MiG-15 in Korea

Top-scoring Canadian Fighter Pilots with the RAF

Flt Lt G F Beurling	31⅓
Wg Cdr V C Woodward	19 & 3 shared
Plt Off W L McKnight	16½
Wg Cdr E J F Charles	15½
Sqn Ldr R A Barton	13 & 6 shared
Wg Cdr J A Kent	13
Wg Cdr P S Turner	11 & 1 shared a.l.

Squadron Code Letters Allocated to RCAF Squadrons Overseas, 1940-45

B – Bomber unit
C – Coastal unit
F – Fighter unit
FB – Fighter-Bomber unit
R – Reconnaissance unit
T – Transport unit

AB	423 (C) Squadron (1943)	OW	426 (B) Squadron
AE	402 (F) Squadron	PT	420 (B) Squadron
AL	429 (B) Squadron	QB	424 (B) Squadron
AN	417 (F) Squadron	QL	413 (C) Squadron
AU	421 (F) Squadron	QO	432 (B) Squadron
BM	433 (B) Squadron	RA	410 (F) Squadron
DB	411 (F) Squadron	RR	407 (C) Squadron
DG	422 (C) Squadron	RU	414 (R) Squadron
DN	416 (F) Squadron	SE	431 (B) Squadron
EE	404 (C) Squadron	SP	400 (R) Squadron
EO	404 (C) Squadron	TH	418 (F/FB) Squadron
EQ	408 (B) Squadron	U6	436 (T) Squadron
F3	438 (FB) Squadron	VR	419 (B) Squadron
GX	415 (C) Squadron (1941-3)	VZ	412 (F) Squadron
G9	430 (R) Squadron	YI	423 (C) Squadron (1944-5)
HU	406 (F) Squadron	YO	401 (F) Squadron
IP	434 (B) Squadron	Y2	442 (F) Squadron
I8	440 (FB) Squadron	ZL	427 (B) Squadron
KH	403 (F) Squadron	Z2	437 (T) Squadron
KP	409 (F) Squadron	2I	443 (F) Squadron
KW	425 (B) Squadron	5V	439 (FB) Squadron
LQ	405 (B) Squadron	6U	415 (B) Squadron (1944-5)
NA	428 (B) Squadron	9G	441 (F) Squadron
NH	415 (C) Squadron (1944)		

THE POSTWAR YEARS

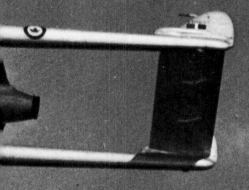

As so often following a war, the strength of the RCAF melted away like snow under a spring sun as soon as the peace came. The first two years following the surrender of Japan were to be a period of transition as the massive forces accumulated by 1945 were steadily demobilized and the armed forces reduced toward a peacetime establishment. Indeed, by the middle of 1946 very little of the once powerful air force remained; in Europe all remaining squadrons had been disbanded, while at home few remained. The bomber force marshaled for service in the Pacific had similarly been reduced to nothing, its Lancaster Xs relegated to storage. 124 (Ferry) Squadron and 428 (Bomber) Squadron remained, but both units were due for disbandment in September 1946. Otherwise just four Regular units continued in service; 12 (Communications) Squadron, 13 and 14 (Photographic) Squadrons would carry on with their duties, while 164 (Transport) Squadron was about to be split into two flights to form the nucleii of two new units which would inherit the numbers 426 and 435.

Plans were afoot to ensure that at least a cadre air force remained,

however, the first post-war assessment being completed in February 1946. This authorized a Regular Air Force of 16,000 men, backed by an Auxiliary of 4500 and a Reserve of 10,000. Eight Regular and 15 Auxiliary squadrons were proposed as the operational arm of this force. All units in the new air force were to be numbered in the 400 series to allow the traditions and history of the famous wartime units to be continued. Initially the air defense and attack capability was to be provided by the Auxiliary units, which at first at any rate, included many fully-trained and experienced wartime aircrew on their strength. Seven of these units had been formed during April 1946 to provide the initial back-up to the more mundane 'bread-and-butter' activities of the handful of Regular units. To replace the remaining aging Hurricanes and Kittyhawks, 100 North American P-51D Mustangs had been ordered from the United States immediately after the end of the war, and these were supplied in the first instance to all but one of these new squadrons; the sole exception was 418 'City of Edmonton' Squadron which was equipped with B-25 Mitchells as a light bomber unit. The new fighter units were:

400 'City of Toronto' Squadron
401 'City of Westmont' Squadron
402 'City of Winnipeg' Squadron
424 'City of Hamilton' Squadron
438 'City of Montreal' Squadron
442 'City of Vancouver' Squadron

Other types were also ordered, principally 90 De Havilland Vampire F-3 jet fighters from the United Kingdom, and 16 Canadair-built Douglas DC-4M North Stars. The latter were special versions of the famous DC 4/6 airliner series, re-engined with four Rolls-Royce Merlins; the order was subsequently supplemented by a further eight purchased from Trans-Canada Airways.

At the end of 1946 the armed forces of Canada were once more united under one Department of Defense, as before the war, but the establishment of the RCAF was revised downward again to 12,735 men. However, a proper command structure was once more initiated, three commands being set up during 1947 as follows:

North-West Air Command, with HQ at Edmonton, Alberta, controlling No 11 Group at Winnipeg and No 12 Group at Vancouver.
Central Air Command, with HQ at Trenton, Ontario, controlling No 10 Group at Halifax and No 9 (Transport) Group.
Maintenance Command, with HQ at Uplands, Ontario.

The last of this trio would later be retitled Air Materiel Command, and the three would be joined in April 1948 by Air Transport Command, formed by expanding No 9 Group. Subsequently North-East and Air Defense Commands would also be formed.

Meanwhile the proposed allocation of squadrons had been

Previous pages: First jet equipment for the RCAF after the war was the De Havilland Vampire fighter.
Below: One of the long-serving Canadair-Douglas DC 4M North Star transports of 426 Squadron, which provided Canada's main contribution to the United Nations effort in Korea.

altered, the Regular air force being increased to ten units, while the Auxiliary force was reduced to a similar number. The Regular element was planned to comprise an Interceptor Wing of two squadrons, initially with Mustangs; a Mobile Tactical wing containing one fighter-bomber and one fighter-reconnaissance squadron – again Mustang-equipped – and an AOP unit; a Transport Wing containing two squadrons of Dakotas; a photographic element, again of two squadrons, and a single bomber-reconnaissance unit mainly for maritime patrol duties. In the event it was to be some months before all these squadrons could be formed and equipped.

In 1947 the Canadian armed forces were finally 'stood down' from their wartime status, but the rebuilding of the new RCAF continued. The remaining original units were renumbered early in the year, 12, 13 and 14 Squadrons becoming 412, 413 and 414 respectively. 412 was destined to continue as a VIP transport and communications unit. It was mainly equipped with Dakotas, but it still had one or two Liberators on hand, although the last of these would be gone before the end of the year. 414 Squadron was likewise Dakota-equipped for its photographic role, although 413 Squadron undertook similar duties with a mixed complement of Mitchells and Lancasters. While this renumbering was in progress, a further Auxiliary unit was formed in the light bomber role, 406 'City of Saskatoon' Squadron being equipped like 418 Squadron with Mitchells. The year also saw the formation of two more Regular units – in June 417 Squadron was formed with Mustangs as the

Tactical Wing's fighter-reconnaissance unit, while in October 444 Squadron came into being also for that Wing, equipped with De Haviland Chipmunk and Auster light aircraft for the AOP role.

The following month, September 1947, saw the arrival of the first of the North Stars, which was issued to 426 Squadron to begin replacing that unit's Dakotas. A major element of modernization occurred six months later with the arrival of the first jet aircraft for service in Canada with the delivery of the Vampires. From March onward these aircraft were issued to 400, 401, 438 and 442 Squadrons, and the Mustangs were consolidated in 402 and 424 Squadrons for fighter-bomber duties. Before the year was out two more Auxiliary units were formed for similar duties with Mustangs – 403 'City of Calgary' and 420 'City of London' Squadrons. The availability of the four Auxiliary fighter-bomber units saw the disbandment of the short-lived 417 Squadron in the Regular force. Just before the end of the year the first of the Regular interceptor squadrons – 410 – was formed with Vampires, and this was to be followed during 1949 by the second such unit when 421 Squadron was formed.

By now, however, the international scene had changed adversely with the marked increase in tension between East and West, culminating in the Berlin Airlift of 1948, and the introduction to contemporary terminology of what Winston Churchill christened 'The Iron Curtain'. A loyal member of the British Commonwealth, and a believer in the necessity of political and military stability in Western

Above: The faithful Dakota was to serve with the RCAF for more than 35 years after the end of WWII.

Below: Chosen as new primary training equipment for production in Canada, the De Havilland Chipmunk saw many years of service.

Above left: Many amphibian versions of the Catalina flyingboat were built in Canada during the war. This is an aircraft of 408 Squadron, in which unit the type supplemented Lancaster 10s.
Left: Avro Lancaster 10-P of 408 Squadron – the RCAF's classic maritime reconnaissance aircraft of the fifties.
Above: First RCAF pilot to shoot down a MiG 15 over Korea while attached to the USAF was Flt Lt J A O Levesque DFC.

homeland. No suitable aircraft capable of operating over the huge areas and in the extreme climates which would be met, was then available for license production.

Not only in the operational field would Canada play her part so generously, but as in 1940-45, in the training role too. A massive new Training Scheme was announced which would train not only the many new aircrew necessary to meet the RCAF's own expansion, but also those of many of the European members of NATO. A new Training Command was formed in April 1949 with headquarters in Trenton, and this was to administer some dozen flying training schools, while each of the flying commands was to set up its own operational training unit. Training was to be on DH (Canada) Chipmunks and Harvard Mark 4s, of which large supplies remained available in store. Most advanced training was to be undertaken in the T-33s, 30 of which were acquired from Lockheed initially, several hundred more following from Canadian lines in the years which followed. Multi-engined training was supplied by 100 Mitchells, while Beech Expeditors remained available in profusion for navigational and other specialized training. Basically this equipment was not to change during the years in which the scheme remained in action.

In the meantime the business of expanding the RCAF with what was available continued. About 30 of the Lancaster 10s (aircraft Mark numbers had been converted from Roman numerals to Arabic after the war) in store were taken out and modified during 1948-49, some to 10-SR standard for air-sea rescue work, others to 10-BR standard for bomber-reconnaissance duties, and some to 10-P standard for photographic work. Subsequently a further 70 would be brought up to 10-MR/MP standard for maritime reconnaissance and patrol as demand for this role grew. The 10-P aircraft went to form 408 Squadron in January 1949 for the photographic role. Formation of this unit allowed the veteran 413 Squadron to have its function changed to that of Survey Transport unit, for which duties it exchanged its remaining Mitchells and Lancasters for Dakotas, Canso amphibians and Norduyn Norsemen. Its life in this new role was to be a short one, however, for it was to be disbanded less than two years later in November 1950. The other old photo squadron, 414, was also struck off at the same time. Another unit to go was 444 AOP Squadron, whose function was no longer required, this unit being disbanded in April 1949, although this latter month saw the birth of a third transport squadron, 436.

The planned bomber-reconnaissance unit – now renamed maritime-reconnaissance – was formed early in 1950, 405 Squadron being equipped with Lancaster 10-MR/MPs; its formation was followed a year later by the similarly equipped 404 Squadron. The confrontations of the 'Cold War' came to a head in June 1950 with the invasion of South Korea by the forces of the North. In the United Nations action which followed, Canada was early in playing her part. RCAF involvement, however, was limited to the despatch of 426 'Thunderbird' Squadron and its new North Stars to McChord Air Force Base, Washington, in July. From here the unit was to maintain a regular air transport service to Japan throughout the war, nearly 600 round trips being completed by 1953, most of them carrying personnel.

Twenty RCAF fighter pilots were also attached to the USAF units in Korea, some of them experienced World War II Spitfire 'jockeys'. Flying Sabres with the 4th and 51st Fighter Interceptor Wings, six of these pilots were to claim a total of ten MiG-15s shot down. The first fell to Flt Lt J A O Levesque, flying with the 334th Squadron of the 4th Wing on 31 March 1951, while the last was claimed on 30 June 1953 by Sqn Ldr John MacKay with the 51st Wing's 39th Squadron. Levesque had claimed four victories during the earlier war, while MacKay had previously been credited with 11 and one shared during that conflict. Another ex-World War II notable, Sqn Ldr James D Lindsay, who had claimed seven victories over Europe, also flew with the 39th Squadron, gaining victories over two MiGs during late 1952. The most successful of the Canadians was Flt Lt Ernest A Glover. Flying with the 334th Squadron, Glover was credited with MiG victories on the 8th, 9th and 16th of September 1952. Sqn Ldr Andrew R Mackenzie, however, an eight victory ace of World War II, and previously commander of the Sabre-flying 441

Europe, Canada took her duty seriously. In December 1948 the Minister of National Defense announced a program of sustained expansion for the Canadian forces due to the 'changing circumstances in international affairs'. No longer would there be a ceiling on the strength of the RCAF; existing airfields would be reconditioned and new ones built, while production of jet aircraft in Canada would be set underway. Initially this would be, as in the past, by way of license production. Aircraft procurement would, however, now be sought more in the United States rather than Britain, since the mutual air defense of the two North American nations would obviously require a high degree of co-operation and interdependence.

The RCAF would now plan for and prepare to undertake three specific roles; the first would be the air defense of the homeland; the second, a major contribution to the new North Atlantic Treaty Organization (NATO) which came into effect in August 1949; the third an involvement when required in any United Nations peace-keeping initiative. To meet the needs of the first two tasks, the indigenous aircraft industry was once more expanded, based on the plants which had performed so handsomely during World War II. Canadair would begin manufacture of the Lockheed T-33A jet trainer – a development of the F-80 Shooting Star fighter, to be known in Canada as the Silver Star. The finest fighter aircraft then available in the West was without doubt the North American F-86 Sabre, and Canadair would also produce this aircraft as the CL-13. The second major producer, Avro Canada, expanded from the Canadian subsidiary of A V Roe of England, would undertake design of a new jet engine, the Orenda, and would design and develop a long-range all-weather interceptor for the defense of the

Above: Sqn Ldr James Lindsay DFC added two MiGs over Korea to seven German aircraft claimed over Europe eight years earlier. He also claimed damage to two more Communist aircraft.
Below: The main jet types chosen for production in Canada for the RCAF during the fifties. Bottom to top: Canadair-Lockheed T-33A Silver Star trainer; Canadair-North American CL-13 Sabre Mk 2 tactical fighter/interceptor; Avro Canada CF-100 Canuck 4 air defense interceptor.

Squadron, was shot down by a MiG-15 and spent the remainder of the war as a prisoner of the Communists.

Soon after the outbreak of the Korean War, the first Canadair-built Sabre Mark 1 flew on 9 August 1950. Production which followed, however, was of the Mark 2, which was upgraded to F-86E standard, and these began to flow off the line during 1951. Meanwhile in October 1950 an eleventh Auxiliary unit had been formed, 411 'County of York' Squadron being equipped with Vampires as was the last Auxiliary unit to be formed, 443 'City of New Westminster' Squadron, when it came into being in September 1951. In 1951 three more Regular fighter squadrons were formed – 416 with Mustangs in January, 441 with Vampires in March, and a similarly-equipped re-formed 413 Squadron in August. This equipment was for work-up only, for just before the year was out all these latter units would have re-equipped with Sabre 2s. Meanwhile, however, 421 Squadron had been despatched to England to undertake a period of operational training with the RAF. Arriving at North Luffenham, Norfolk, without aircraft, the squadron was temporarily equipped with borrowed RAF Vampire F5 and Meteor T7 aircraft, which it flew until its return to Canada later in the year.

In February 1951 a revised expansion program had been announced, allowing for an increase in personnel to 42,000 and a strength of 41 Regular and Reserve (Auxiliary) Squadrons to be achieved by 1953. One element of this expansion was the formation in June 1951 of the Air Defense Command, and within this No 1 (Fighter) OTU had been set up at Chatham, New Brunswick, to train pilots for No 1 Air Division, which was to be the RCAF's contribution to NATO. The first squadron to receive the Sabre was 410 'Cougar', followed by the recently formed 441 'Silver Fox', and 439 'Tiger' Squadron which was formed on 1 September. The discarded Vampires of 410 and 441 Squadrons went to keep the Auxiliary fighter units up to strength. These three units were to form No 1 Wing, which was set up at North Luffenham in England on 1 November 1951, a base handed over to the RCAF by the RAF.

The Sabres of 410 and 441 Squadrons were cocooned against sea spray, and transported across the Atlantic before the end of the year. This was not to be the way in which following units would come, however, and it was left to 439 Squadron – not ready as soon as the older units – to pioneer the new route. On 30 May 1952 the unit's Sabres began Operation 'Leapfrog', flying from Bagotville, PQ, to Goose Bay, Labrador, and from there via Bluie West One, Greenland to Keflavik, Iceland, and on to RAF Kinloss in Scotland for the last leg to North Luffenham. Delayed en route by bad weather, the 21 fighters arrived safely on 15 June to bring No 1 Wing to its full strength.

Above: Early production Sabre Mk 2 in flight prior to issue to an operational unit.

Meanwhile No 2 Wing had begun preparation. Following its return from England, 421 'Red Indian' Squadron received its Sabres during December 1951, as did 416 'Lynx' Squadron, which passed its Mustangs to the Auxiliaries. The Wing was brought up to strength with the formation during November of 430 'Silver Falcon' Squadron. Training completed, the Wing was to follow 439 Squadron across the Atlantic air route to take up base at Gros Tenquin in France, where it became a part of 4th Allied Tactical Air Force (4 ATAF) in October 1952. 413 'Tusker' Squadron exchanged its Vampires for Sabres during summer 1952, while 427 'Lion' and 434 'Blue Nose Sailboat' Squadrons were formed at this time as the balance of the establishment of No 3 Wing. Toward the end of the year 414 'Black Knight' Squadron re-formed, followed by 422 'Tomahawk', and, on 1 March 1953, 444 'Cobra' Squadron, the twelfth and last of the Sabre units, to complete No 4 Wing. Following completion of training No 3 Wing flew across to its European base at Zweibrücken, Germany, early in 1953, while No 4 Wing reached Söllingen, near Baden Baden, in September.

All No 1 Air Division was now in Europe, and divisional head-quarters was established at Metz in an old chateau. For equipment back-up No 3 Air Materiel Base was set up in England at Langar, and a small air transport component was formed for communication with the bases in France and Germany; to equip this some Expeditors were shipped across, while three Bristol Freighter Mk 31s were purchased locally.

Before formation of the Division had been completed, the Sabre 2 had been superseded in production by the Mark 4 – the first Canadair Sabre powered by an Orenda engine. With its 300-odd aircraft, the Division formed a major part of NATO air defense and was better equipped at the time than any other element apart from the USAF's F-86F Wings. Main duties included patroling the frontier with East Germany, and maintaining armed 'Zulu' alert, on standby for scrambles to intercept unidentified 'bandits'.

Even as the Sabre program was reaching fulfillment, the formation of the first home-defense interceptor units to receive the powerful new Avro Canada CF-100 all-weather fighters was approaching. After initial testing of the prototype CF-100s, a small batch of unarmed Mark 2s was produced on a pre-production basis during 1952, these being employed not only for further tests, but also for initial training on the type at the new No 3 (All-Weather) OTU formed at Cold Lake.

The first fully operational Mark 3 flew before the end of 1952, armed with eight 0.50in Browning machine guns in a retractable under-fuselage tray. Production of 70 began, the first of these going to Cold Lake, where they were used to form the first of the new interceptor units on 1 April 1953 – 445 Squadron. Other squadrons followed, 423 'Bald Eagle' forming at St Hubert, PQ, in June and 440 at Bagotville, PQ, in November. The more sophisticated Mark 4 came into production in 1954, featuring an improved APG 40 airborne gun-laying radar and a Hughes MG 2 fire control system. This version of the Canuck, as it had become named (although it was known more familiarly to its crews as the 'Clunk'), also had a revised armament; in place of wingtip fuel tanks a pod could be carried on each wingtip containing 29 unguided 2.75in (70mm) folding fin aircraft rockets (FFARs), which could be carried in addition to, or as an alternative to the gun pack. Some 137 of these aircraft were built, followed from November by 190 more Mark 4Bs, powered by up-rated Orendas and with provision for the under-fuselage gun pack to be replaced by an optional alternative tray carrying more FFARs. 1954 was very much the year of the CF-100, no less than 55 percent of total defense funds being allocated to the program. Before

Above: North American P-51D Mustangs of 416 Squadron seen in echelon formation on 24 January 1952. Only the fourth aircraft carries the unit codes, AS, and the individual letter N.
Below: Sabre Mk 2s of No 4 Wing, aircraft of 414 'Black Knight' squadron in the foreground, at Ottawa in 1953 prior to departing for Europe.

Above: Mustang fighter-bomber in flight. The code letters have not been identified.
Above right: CF-104 Starfighter in flight.

the year was over six more squadrons had been formed to bring Air Defense Command to its full complement of nine. These were:

409 'Nighthawk' Squadron	428 'Ghost' Squadron
419 'Moose' Squadron	432 'Panther' Squadron
425 'Alouette' Squadron	433 'Porcupine' Squadron

423, 440 and 445 Squadrons were also re-equipped with Mark 4s, and by mid-1955 281 examples of this variant were on hand.

The CF-100s also played a major part in the development of Canada's own air-launched guided missile, Velvet Glove. More than 300 test shots with this missile were made from CF-100s and Sabres during the period 1954-56, a guided weapon being viewed as a more effective armament for the planned Mark 6 model of the Canuck, but in the event the US-built Sperry Sparrow II was considered to be better and plans were eventually made to build the latter under license as an alternative – plans which were not in the event to come to fruition, as will be seen.

Existing squadrons were not being neglected while all this new equipment was being acquired. Forty-eight Fairchild C-119F transports had been ordered from the US. The first of these replaced 435 Squadron's Dakotas in September 1952, while 436 Squadron re-equipped during the following April. These new aircraft would be modified up to C-119G standard in 1954. For its VIP duties 412

Above: CF-100 Mark 3 aircraft soon after entering service in 1952.
Below: Replacement for the Sabre was the Canadair CF-104 version of the famous Lockheed F-104G Starfighter.

Squadron had received a single Canadair C-5 (radial-engined version of the North Star), while in 1953 two De Havilland Comet 1A airliners were added to its existing establishment of Dakotas and Expeditors.

Two further new air commands were also formed in 1953. Maritime was to control the growing strength of the patrol squadrons, and Tactical – both formed in June. The latter would control the Auxiliary squadrons and the search and rescue units, and could, when necessary, have the C-119 squadrons of Air Transport Command attached to it. Search and rescue remained a vital and important role in Canada's wilds. These duties were still being undertaken by Lancasters, Dakotas, Cansos and Norsemen, but during 1953 the first helicopters were introduced to this role with the acquisition of some Vertol H-21As. Air Transport Command was also now acquiring some helicopters, including six H-21Cs, ten H-19s (Sikorsky S55s), six H-34As (S58s) and a number of Bell 47Gs and Sikorsky S51s; these were operated by 108 Communications Flight.

For the maritime role Canadair was developing a version of the Bristol Brittania airliner, extensively converted and fitted with Wright 981 radial engines in place of the British aircraft's turbo-props. This advanced aircraft would be the ultimate replacement of

the Lancaster, but would not be available for some years. Consequently in 1955 25 Lockheed P2V-7 Neptunes were acquired to re-equip 404 and 405 Squadrons, while 407 Squadron, which had been formed in the West at Comox, BC, in July 1952, soldiered on with the faithful Lancaster; a few of the Neptunes went to the Maritime OTU.

Development of the fighter aircraft continued, and during 1954 the Sabre 5 was introduced, 370 of which were built with an up-rated Orenda 10. In October No 1 Overseas Ferry Unit was formed to fly these over to Europe to replace the earlier Mark 2s and 4s in the Air Division. Early in 1955 No 1 Wing moved from North Luffenham to Marville in France. The British airfield continued to be used by the North Stars which maintained the communication and logistics link between the Division and home.

The CF-100 was also further developed, and the Mark 5 replaced the 4B in production late in 1955. This new aircraft featured an elongated wing and other refinements. The last 50 Mark 4Bs were upgraded to Mark 5 standard on the production line, and were followed by 275 more Mark 5s between then and the end of 1958. During 1955 meanwhile three CF-100s had been flown over to North Luffenham on detachment for exercises with the RAF.

By now the RCAF had reached its planned strength of 41 squad-

Above: The fully-developed, missile-armed CF-100 Mark 4.
Below: One of two De Havilland Comet IAs acquired for 412 Squadron in 1953 as VIP transports.

Below: Sabre 5 carrying the new camouflage developed for all RCAF European-based operational aircraft.

rons, and employed 2968 aircraft of 21 types, while Regular personnel strength had risen to 49,500 men. During the year 25 CCF-built Beech T-34A Mentors were acquired for the Air Training Command to replace some of the aging Harvards, but these were not found to offer any great improvement, and were subsequently sold to Turkey.

The introduction of the ultimate Sabre, the Mark 6, took place in 1956. This featured an Orenda 14 engine and an extended, slatted '6-3' leading edge to the wing. No 1 OFU ferried these across to the Air Division, taking back the Mark 5s to Canada. Here the latter were issued in October to 401 and 438 Squadrons of the Auxiliary force to supplement their Vampires, 400, 411, 442 and 443 Squadrons also being recipients over the following months. Each of these units was to employ about eight Sabres, together with a number of Vampires, T-33s and Harvard 4s. However, at this time 420 'City of London' Squadron was disbanded.

The pilots of the Air Division were more than happy with their new mounts, which were probably the best of all the Sabres built, and were undoubtedly one of the best fighters then available in Europe. They took a delight in 'bouncing' USAF F-86Fs, over which they had a distinct edge, and indeed they were a match for all the new swept-wing types joining NATO squadrons at the time – the F-84F Thunderstreaks of the fighter-bomber squadrons, the Mystere IVs of the Armée de l'Air, and the RAF's Hunters. The only fighters which could outmaneuver them in a dogfight were the RAF Venoms of 2 ATAF – and these were inferior in every other respect.

There was, however, one way in which the Air Division was deficient – as was the rest of NATO at this time: all-weather capacity was lacking. As soon as the daylight disappeared, or the weather 'socked-in', the 'Swords' – as the Sabres were known in the RCAF – were tied to the ground. Apart from the RAF's short-ranging all-weather Meteors and Venoms, there was nothing – Javelins and Vautours were not yet available in quantity – and the Canadians were requested to incorporate an all-weather element into their commitment. Following the recent North Luffenham detachment, the CF-100s already had experience of the Atlantic crossing, and consequently in November 1956 445 Squadron – the original Canuck unit – flew its Mark 4Bs across to Marville to join No 1 Wing as the start of Operation 'Nimble Bat'. With the arrival of the new unit, 410 Squadron left the Wing and flew home to Canada. Thereafter 423 Squadron replaced 416 in No 2 Wing, 440 replaced 413 in No 3 and

Above: Sabre 5s in 1954. The aircraft in the background carries the AS codes of 416 Squadron.
Right: A CF-100 Mark 5 salvoes the wingtip-mounted battery of 2.75in FFARs.
Below right: The ultimate production version of the CF-100 – the Mark 5.

419 replaced 414 in No 4, the changeover being completed by mid-1957. On reaching Canada, the four Sabre squadrons were deactivated and re-formed with CF-100 Mark 5s to take the place of the four units now in Europe. Other Mark 5s replaced the earlier models in the remaining five home defense units, and the four squadrons with the Air Division retained their Mark 4Bs. The spare Sabre 6s went to the Auxiliary fighter squadrons, and No 1 (Fighter) OTU retained these aircraft for several more years as a result. No 1 OFU, however, was disbanded in 1957 after the last Mark 6 had been delivered to Europe.

In October 1956 war broke out in the Middle East following the Suez crisis, and on the conclusion of hostilities a United Nations peacekeeping force was established in the Sinai Desert, between the Israeli and Egyptian forces. Canadian troops were to form a part of this Emergency Force from the start, and were flown to the area in 426 Squadron's North Stars. The C-119s of 435 Squadron, joined by a detachment from 436 Squadron, were then flown over to the area to aid in providing logistic support to the force, using Capodichino airfield, just outside Naples in Italy, as their base. Early in 1957 the squadrons returned to Canada, but two detachments were left behind which would serve the UN forces for a considerably longer time. These were 114 Communications Flight at Capodichino with four C-119s, and 115 Communications Flight based at El Arish in the Canal Zone, and equipped with three Dakotas and four DHC Otters. When the UN became involved in the Congo situation a few years later 426 Squadron would again serve.

The end of 1957 was to see delivery of the first Canadair Argus to the Maritime Air Command, and 13 Mark 1s and 20 Mark 2s were constructed over the following months. Initially these aircraft were to join 404 and 405 Squadrons, replacing the few remaining Lancasters still with these units, and flying alongside the Neptunes – although it was to be 1958/9 before sufficient were on hand for either unit to start relinquishing any of the American aircraft. The Neptunes were then gradually transferred across the country to 407 Squadron at Comox, first by 405 Squadron and then by 404. By 1960

both these units had completed full re-equiment with the newer aircraft.

Other changes were afoot, however. By the end of 1956 the remaining Mustangs with the fighter-bomber units of the Auxiliary air force had finally been declared obsolete, and at the beginning of 1957, 402, 403 and 424 Squadrons were all re-equipped with Expeditors, becoming light transport units. This was only the start of a major change of emphasis for the Auxiliaries as a whole. In March 1958 the two light bomber squadrons, 406 and 418, also became light transport units, while in October of that year the whole force ceased its operational involvement, and the Sabres, T-33s and Vampires were handed in by 400, 401, 411, 438, 442 and 443 Squadrons. Because of the increasing complexity of modern technology it had not proved possible to re-equip the essentially 'part time' squadrons with all-weather interceptors to take their place more fully in the Air Defense Command role. The situation appeared more likely to worsen than improve, and as there was little requirement for tactical fighter or fighter-bomber units in the homeland, the decision was taken to allot them a simpler and perhaps more immediately useful task. All would now become light transport and rescue squadrons, equipped in each case with a mixed complement of Expeditors and Otters. Thus at a stroke the whole character of the Auxiliary Air Force was changed.

The next year was a watershed of major change for the RCAF. On 12 May the US-Canadian Air Defense Agreement was signed, whereby the nine home squadrons of CF-100s were contributed to the North American Air Defense Command (NORAD), the joint Headquarters of which was based at Colorado Springs in the USA. This command is based on three concentric lines of radar stations, the last of which – the DEW (Distant Early Warning) Line was completed during 1958 along the length of the Arctic coastline from Alaska to Greenland. Behind this is the Mid Canada Line (or 'McGill Fence') which follows the 55th Parallel, and then the 'Pinetree' Line – the final line around the industrial area of Eastern North America. 'Pinetree' was a joint US/Canadian manned operation; the McGill Fence was wholly Canadian, while the DEW Line was US-manned and maintained.

Early in the fifties Avro Canada had begun development of a

supersonic all-weather fighter to replace the CF-100, and this had first flown in March 1958. The massive twin-engined delta-winged CF-105 Arrow proved to be one of the largest, fastest and most sophisticated aircraft in the world at the time. The initial Mark 1 prototype was powered by Pratt and Whitney J57 engines, but the production Mark 2 was to have Canadian Iroquois engines, developed from the successful Orenda series, and was to be armed with license-built Sparrow II missiles. Initially it was envisaged that 500-600 would be built to re-equip all nine home defense squadrons, and 11 Auxiliary units, but escalating costs and complexity soon showed this to be unrealistic.

Indeed, no sooner had the Arrow flown than it was surrounded by controversy. It was clearly too expensive for a nation the size of Canada, and unless export orders of a substantial nature could be achieved, the burden would be crippling. In the event, such orders were not forthcoming. Initially 32 CF-105s were ordered for continued development, but by the end of 1958 the development of the aircraft's weapons systems was canceled, and cancelation of the whole program soon followed, with near fatal results for Avro

Canada and the engine manufacturers. It marked the end of major military aircraft design and development in Canada.

Of equal significance, however, was the decision by John Diefenbaker's government that the day of the manned defensive interceptor was over, and that the gap would be filled by the acquistion of Boeing IM-99B Bomarc anti-bomber guided missiles from the United States. This was a fashionable belief in the late fifties, shared notably by Duncan Sandys' Defense Ministry in London, and was to have unfortunate repercussions on several air forces, not least the RCAF and RAF. The CF-100 Mark 6 missile-carrier had been canceled at the start of 1958, and with the cancelation, too, of the Sparrow II, the gradual decline of the RCAF had been set in train, despite an increase in orders for the existing CF-100 Mark 5, which was, of course, nothing more than a stop-gap. In the event the Bomarc program was to prove disappointing and protracted, and the missile was never to take its envisaged full place in the defenses.

Initially it would not have appeared that the RCAF was about to decline, for 1958 had seen it reach a peak peacetime strength of over 56,000 men with more than 3000 aircraft; indeed at the start of the

Below: Queen of the Skies! The classic Canadair Sabre 6, probably the finest Sabre variant ever built.

Above left: Lockheed P2V-7 Neptune – the maritime 'stop-gap' between the Lancaster and the Argus.
Above: The faithful Beech C-45 Expeditor light transport.
Left: In latter years remaining Buffalos have been modified for the general role, and now serve alongside the Twin Otters of 440 Squadron.

year there had been some 600 jet combat aircraft on hand, serving with 21 Regular and six Auxiliary squadrons, from a total of 29 Regular and ten Auxiliary units. New equipment, too, was still forthcoming in plenty, ranging across all aspects of the air force's establishment. Early in 1958 30 Ryan Firebee high speed target drones had been acquired, while in mid-1959 an order was placed for ten Grumman UF-2 Albatros amphibians for the search and rescue role. 412 Squadron received some more modern equipment for its VIP transport role when ten Canadair CL-66 Cosmopolitans were ordered. These were developments of the Convair 440 Metropolitan airliner, re-engined with Rolls-Royce Eland turboprops. Further transport equipment was in view with the first flight of the Canadair CL-44-6 Yukon, eight of which were ordered as the CC-106 for the RCAF. Like the Argus, this was a development of the Brittania, featuring a 'stretched' fuselage some 12 feet longer, the tail of which was sideways-hinged to allow for easy loading of large consignments; it was also up-engined with Rolls-Royce Tyne turoprops. In 1960 the order would be increased to 12.

Most important decision of 1959 was to be the selection of a successor to the Sabre to serve with the Air Division in Europe. It had been decided to alter the RCAF function here from that of fighter, to low level attack, and at first consideration was given to a two-seat subsonic type, capable of delivering conventional or nuclear weapons within a range up to 1000 miles. By September, however, the choice had been made of the Lockheed F-104G Starfighter, to be built under license by Canadair, but in the attack configuration, rather than in its designed fighter role.

More transport aircraft were acquired in 1960, the first of 19 Lockheed C-130 Hercules being issued to 435 Squadron, the remaining C-119s being consolidated in 436. Five DHC-4 Caribou light transports were also purchased as the CC-108, and three of these subsequently replaced the Dakotas with 115 Flight with the UN in 1964.

Now, however, the Bomarc program was giving many problems, and during 1960 three-quarters of this was to be abandoned, leaving the RCAF with a major problem of defense modernization. There was no alternative but to 'buy American' again, and orders were placed in June 1961 for 54 of the two-seat F-101B version of the McDonnell Voodoo fighter, plus ten dual control F-101Fs. These were funded by way of an agreement with the US Government that in return for their supply, Canada would take over the manning and maintenance of 16 of the DEW Line radar stations on Canadian soil, and would also contribute $10 million to the cost of an additional 150 F-104s to be built by Canadair to full fighter standard for other NATO nations. The first CF-104 for the RCAF flew on 14 August 1961, some 200 being on order for the Air Division.

The CF-100s soldiered on as an important part of NORAD, joining on occasion in USAF programs far from their normal area of operation. Two were assigned to one such venture, Operation 'Lookout', joining USAF interceptors based on Ascension Island in the South Atlantic to undertake interceptions of ICBM nosecaps during test firings; this detachment lasted 11 months. Later three more were attached to Patrick Air Force Base, Florida, for joint tests and exercises. During April 1961, however, to reduce operating costs and maintain the life of the remaining aircraft by keeping a substantial proportion of the force in storage, 413, 428, 432 and 433 Squadrons were disbanded. Their place was partially taken later in the year when 446 Squadron was formed at North Bay as the first Bomarc unit; the second – 447 – would be formed a year later, but these would be the only two.

Other new squadrons were forming at this time, however, for in May 1961 a fourth maritime-reconnaissance squadron, 415, was formed on the east coast, equipped from the start with the Argus, while in October 437 Squadron came into existence with the first production Yukons, to undertake a transatlantic service to Europe. More helicopters were also on the way, three additional Hiller UH-12Es being ordered for the training role together with six Boeing Vertol 107-IIs (to be known as CH-113s) to be delivered in 1962 for the search and rescue role.

In November 1961 the first CF-101B Voodoos were available at Namao, Edmonton, where 410 Squadron began conversion. It was to be followed at six weekly intervals by 409, 414, 416 and 425 Squadrons. The Voodoo was initially to carry Hughes AIM-4D Falcon guided missiles, later supplemented by unguided, nuclear-

Above: De Havilland Canada DHC-3 Otter, a ubiquitous light transport seen here fitted with floats. These aircraft were acquired mainly for the re-equipment of the Auxilliary Air Force units for their new light transport role.
Below: DHC-3 Otter in standard form.

tipped AIR-2A Genies. Delivery of the CF-104 was not far behind, 70 having been completed by April 1962. Early in the year the first two-seater CF-104Ds were delivered to a new unit, No 6 Strike Reconnaissance OTU at Cold Lake. Delivery to Europe of the operational version, due in November, was running late as the year progressed, but beginning in October, 137 were delivered disassembled in the capacious fuselages of 435 Squadron's C-130s. The first was issued to 427 Squadron in No 3 Wing at Zweibrücken. No replacement was considered for the four squadrons of CF-100 Mark 4Bs in Europe, however, and these were withdrawn in early 1963, flying back to Canada where they were disbanded (419, 423, 440 and 445 Squadrons). Thus within a period of less than two years the Air Division had been reduced from 12 squadrons to eight, and Air Defense Command from nine squadrons to five – at least insofar as manned aircraft were concerned. Production of the 200th and last CF-104 was due to be completed in April 1963, but in the event was delayed until June to keep the line open for the MDAP order for NATO.

More CL-44 Yukons were delivered during 1962, some joining 412 Squadron. The availability of these new aircraft allowed the faithful North Stars to be retired after a most distinguished career,

and in September the long-serving 426 Squadron disbanded. Another familiar type to disappear at this time was the B-25 Mitchell, and the last of these still in use as navigational and radar trainers was withdrawn during the year. However, three more CC-109 Cosmopolitans were ordered to supplement the ten in service, and the Canadair CL-41 jet trainer flew; it would be favorably considered by the RCAF which placed an order in 1963 for 190 to enter service during 1965 as a primary and basic trainer.

As is the way with military aircraft, no sooner are they in service than it is time to consider their successor, and by the end of 1963 consideration was already being given to the possibility of replacement of the CF-101B by the F-4 Phantom – consideration which in the event was to continue for many years.

By the start of 1964 Canada was at the first of a string of financial crises, and the year began for the RCAF with a cut of $70 million in the Defense Budget. An additional 24 two-seat CF-104Ds had been ordered, but this number was now cut to 16, and was to be achieved by purchase of more Lockheed-built aircraft. The Reserve was also to be cut from 2220 to 860, and this would mean Auxiliary units would also have to be cut. The short straw was drawn by 403 Squadron, which was disbanded forthwith.

Previous spread: A trio of Lockheed C-130 Hercules – the hardy perennials of the transport force.

As 28 nuclear warheads had now arrived for the Bomarcs of 446 Squadron at North Bay, and 28 more were due soon for 447 Squadron at La Macaza, Quebec, the opportunity was taken to use this as an excuse for disbanding two CF-101B squadrons at these locations, 410 at Ottawa going in April and 414 at North Bay in June. Sixty of the original Voodoo delivery were still available, however, and were used for keeping the other three squadrons up to strength. April also saw the end of service for the last of the RCAF's really old types when 408 Squadron handed in its last three Lancaster 10-PRs, then moving from Rockcliffe to Uplands to become a transport unit. Dakotas were received initially, but were soon followed by C-119s and some T-33s. A year later both this unit and 436 Squadron would be re-equipped with C-130s, and the day of the C-119 would also be at an end.

These reductions had not been enough, however, and April 1964 brought more cuts for Financial Year 64/65. This time two utility squadrons were each to be reduced in strength by six fixed wing aircraft and two helicopters, while the RCAF's aerobatic team, the 'Golden Hawks', with its gold-painted Sabre 6s, was to be disbanded.

The main source of concern rested with the Air Division, however. By the end of 1963 ten CF-104s had been lost in accidents in Europe, but requests for replacement strike aircraft had been turned down. It was now clear that to maintain eight squadrons at an 18 aircraft strength would not be easy. In an effort to ease the situation, the strength of the Cold Lake OTU was reduced from 70 to 30 aircraft, and the balance – including most of the 38 CF-104Ds – was distributed to the European-based squadrons.

There were other problems too. In the climate of de Gaulle's France, the French government had now refused to allow foreign-controled nuclear weapons to be based on their soil. In consequence it was decided to convert half of the Air Division to the non-nuclear attack role, the CF-104s being modified to carry 20mm Vulcan cannon and conventional stores of bombs and missiles. No 2 Wing at

Above: Grumman UF-2 Albatros light amphibian flyingboat of the search and rescue service.
Below: The Avro Canada CF-105 Arrow interceptor prototype – the last major Canadian-designed warplane to be built.

Far left: The RCAF's 'Snow Bird' Aerobatic Team formate in their Canadair CL-41 Tutors.
Near left: DHC-4 Caribou, four of which were initially acquired as the CC-108 to serve with 115 Flight as part of Canada's commitment to the United nations Peacekeeping Forces.
Below: Canadair CL-66 Cosmopolitan, a licence-built Rolls-Royce Eland-powered development of the Convair 440 Metropolitan, employed by 412 Squadron during the sixties as the CC-109 VIP transport.

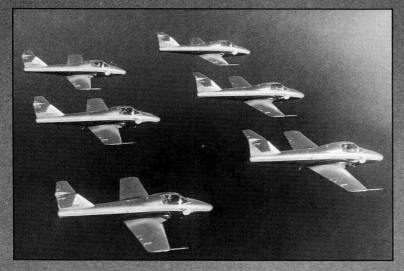

Below: The mighty Canadair CL-44-6 Yukon transport, developed from the Bristol Brittania. These aircraft served with 412 and 437 Squadrons as the CC-106.
Above left: After a long delay, the CL-41 Tutor was ordered in quantity for the RCAF as the CT-114 trainer.
Above: One of the last North American B-25 Mitchells; these light bombers were employed for many years by the RCAF as navigational trainers.

Gros Tenquin was closed down, 421 Squadron joining No 4 Wing at Baden-Söllingen, and 430 Squadron went to No 3 Wing at Zweibrücken, while No 1 Wing at Marville was converted to the reconnaissance role. Strength was thus now:

No 1 Wing, Marville	No 2 Wing, Zweibrücken	No 3 Wing, Baden-Söllingen
439 Squadron	427 Squadron	421 Squadron
441 Squadron	430 Squadron	422 Squadron
	434 Squadron	444 Squadron

During the latter part of the year consideration was given to a replacement for the CF-104, initial investigations identifying the Spey-engined F-4 Phantom, Northrop F-5A, Republic F-105, North American F-111A, Grumman A-6A Intruder, Vought A-7A Corsair, the A-5, or as an outsider, the North American F-100S development of the old Super Sabre. Opposition from the Army and Navy to the Phantom, due to its cost and excessive sophistication, caused the RCAF defensively to reduce its requirement from 218 to 100 aircraft in answer. Early in 1965 the F-5A was provisionally selected, although some consideration was also given to a version of the well-proven McDonnell-Douglas A-4 Skyhawk. As the year progressed it was decided that the aircraft should, as before, be license-produced by Canadair, but the RCAF's requirement for 200 CF-5s was whittled down to 130-135 by the summer, and when an intention to order was announced in September, it had shrunk to 125. In the event, only 115 were to be built.

Meanwhile other re-equipment continued. Early in 1965 four additional C-130E Hercules were ordered, as were 15 DHC Buffalo STOL tactical transports. When delivery of the latter began in 1967, a new unit, 429 'Bison' Squadron, was formed to operate them. During 1966 seven Dassault Fan-Jet Falcon high-speed communications and light transport aircraft were ordered from France for 412 Squadron, with an option for an additional 13. During 1967 seven of this squadron's 13 CC-109 Cosmopolitans were re-engined with Alison T-56 turboprops to extend their useful life.

During its service with NATO the F-104 Starfighter had acquired a considerable notoriety due to the heavy attrition suffered by several air forces in accidents – notably the West German Luftwaffe. Much of the reason for this was not directly connected with the aircraft itself, but it is fair to say that CF-104 attrition in the RCAF had been higher than average, and by the end of 1967 had reached 44 aircraft – nearly a quarter of the total. During the year, to keep up the strength of the other units, No 3 and 4 Wings had each been reduced by one squadron, 434 and 444 Squadrons being disbanded in March and April respectively.

During the year, however, two new units had been formed in Canada. Following the withdrawal from front-line service of the CF-100s, an investigation of the aircraft remaining on hand had shown that the airframe life of these was double what had originally been believed, and much flying time remained in the considerable quantity of Canucks still available. No 3 (AW) OTU was not therefore disbanded, and continued to operate at Bagotville until May 1964, by which time it had trained over 1000 crews. It then set up an

Electronic Warfare Unit employing 14 CF 100 Mark 5C and D fighters and 15 T-33s, which provided radar targeting for both Canadian and USAF interceptors undertaking practice interceptions. In 1967 this unit was renamed 414 'Black Knight' Squadron, while 148 Squadron was formed as a Technical Evaluation unit.

On 1 February 1968 a major change took place when the three military services were combined as the Canadian Armed Forces. RCAF ranks were replaced by those of the Army, as were the blue uniforms, and all units in each command became administered by that command. The commands were much as they had been within the RCAF – Maritime, Mobile and Air Defense, with Air Transport and Training now one combined command. Maritime now included the remaining squadrons of the Royal Canadian Navy's air service, while Mobile included the greater part of the Army. The forces in Europe formed a separate Canadian Forces Europe command.

This unification was introduced to reduce costs – something which failed to happen, the main result being a steady decline in the morale of the servicemen – already depressed by years of financial stringency – and by a growing pressure for de-unification. The air elements now included in the force which had not previously been a part of the RCAF were the DHC-built Grumman CS2F-1 Trackers of the Navy, together with a number of helicopter units from both the Navy and the Army, and Army Cessna light aircraft. The RCN had originally possessed a relatively substantial air arm based on the aircraft carrier HMCS *Bonaventure* and on the land base at Shearwater, which had comprised two squadrons of McDonnell F2H-3 Banshee fighters and three of Trackers, plus a sizable helicopter force. The fighters had already gone, and the other units were reduced considerably following the withdrawal of the carrier.

In June 1968 the first CF-5A was delivered, but in the event these were not to be used to replace the Air Division CF-104s, as two new tactical units were formed in Canada as 433 and 434 Squadrons within Mobile Command. During 1969 three Canadair CX-84 V/STOL aircraft were ordered for test purposes in the rescue, evacuation, photographic and general purpose role, while in November 50 Bell CUH-1N helicopters were ordered, with options on another 20. A statement in parliament during the summer had indicated the great reduction in size of the air forces, which now possessed little more than a third of the numbers available a decade before. By now the last of the Neptunes had been replaced by Argus aircraft, and it was notable that already these aircraft had disappeared from the inventory, together with all Sabres and C-119s, as well as the older types such as North Stars, Harvards, Lancasters, Mitchells and Mustangs.

Above: McDonnell CF-101B Voodoo air defense interceptors at North Bay.

Air Strength in 1968

Fighter/Attack	
CF-104 Starfighter	183
CF-101 Voodoo	60
CF-5	10
CF-100 Canuck	43

Transport	
CC-106 Yukon	12
C-130 Hercules	23
CC-109 Cosmopolitan	9
C-45 Expeditor	53
C-47 Dakota	76
CC-115 Buffalo	15
CC-108 Caribou	8
Dassault Fan-Jet Falcon	7

Maritime Reconnaissance	
CP-107 Argus	32
CS2F Tracker	69
CHS-52 Sea King	38

Rescue/Helicopter/Liaison	
CH-113A Voyageur	9
CH-112 Nomad	20
CH-113 Labrador	6
CUH-1H Iroquois	10
DHC-3 Otter	38
Cessna L-19/L-193	24
Vertol H-21	6
Vertol H-44	4
Sikosrsky HO-45	5
Sikorsky H-34	3
CSR-110 Albatros	9

Trainers	
DHC-1 Chipmunk	51
CT-114 Tutor	179
T-33 Silver Star	213

Against this background of reduced strength came a shock for NATO when in July 1969 plans were announced to withdraw the six squadrons of CF-104s from Europe, starting in 1970. Strong reaction was forthcoming, and although the Canadians proposed that in an emergency the Mobile Command CF-5A squadrons could be switched to Europe swiftly by using air-refueling (three squadrons of these aircraft were envisaged at this point), they were subsequently prevailed upon to take less drastic action. Consequently at the end of the year plans for the early seventies were announced which set the scene for what was to follow:

Canadian Forces Europe: at an early date three of the remaining six CF-104 units would be disbanded, leaving 421, 439 and 441 Squadrons at Baden-Söllingen, two to undertake the strike role and one for reconnaissance. No 1 Air Division would become No 1 Canadian Air Group, Lahr airfield also being retained as an airfield for the ex-Army helicopter element. The nuclear role of the CF-104s would end in January 1972.

Maritime Command: the Trackers and Sea Kings would continue to serve, but a replacement would be sought for the Argus in 404, 405, 407 and 415 Squadrons during 1973.

Mobile Command: the Bagotville-based CF-5A unit, being in the heart of French-speaking Canada, would be known as 433ᵉ Esca-

drille tactique de combat; there would only be one other CF-5A unit, 434 Squadron at Cold Lake. Four new Utility Tactical Transport Helicopter Flights would be formed when the Bell CUH-1Ns were delivered, while the helicopter OTU was now to be numbered 403 Squadron. 408 Squadron, having relinquished its transport role, would operate T-33s at Rivers. A new squadron, 450 (Transport Helicopter), would operate the Voyageur helicopters at Namao/Trenton.

Air Defense Command: there would be no change. Three CF-101 units (409 Squadron at Comox, 416 Squadron at Chatham and 425 Squadron at Bagotville) and two Bomarc units (446 Squadron at North Bay and 447 Squadron at La Macaza) would remain, as would 414 ECM Squadron with CF-100s and T-33s at Uplands. The CF-104 OTU at Cold Lake now became 417 OT Squadron, and the CF-101 and T-33 OTU at Bagotville and Chatham, became 410 OT Squadron.

Air Transport and Training Command: air transport was to be reduced to four squadrons; 412 Squadron with seven Falcons; 437 Squadron with four Yukons; 435 and 436 Squadrons operating a pool of 23 C-130s. In Training Command 53 C-45s and 23 Dakotas were due for retirement during 1970-72. The six Air Reserve squadrons were to be reorganized, each with five Otters – 401 and 438 Squadrons at Montreal, 400 and 411 Squadrons at Toronto, 402 Squadron at Winnipeg and 418 Squadron at Edmonton.

Generally this program was to be followed with only minor changes taking place. In April 1970 four Boeing 707-320C jets were ordered for 437 Squadron to undertake the dual role of transports and tankers, while in June an order for 74 Bell Textron Kiowa helicopters was placed for light observation duties. In August an unusual swap was arranged whereby the surviving 58 CF-101s were exchanged for 58 ex-USAF F-101Fs, plus eight additional aircraft to bring the force up to its original strength. These improved aircraft were superior on all counts to the old CF-101Bs, particularly at low level.

Later in the year yet further cuts were made which mainly affected the CF-5As. Some 74 of the 115 were put into storage, and any question of forming two further squadrons as had been hoped, were quashed. Twenty of the 74 were earmarked for attrition, but the other 54 were to be put up for sale – and indeed were subsequently sold to Venezuela. At the same time the bases at Rivers, Gimli and Manitoba were closed down. Despite this cutback, the two existing CF-5A squadrons were able to undertake their first detachment to Europe in October 1970 for a month's operational trials, flying the close support, armed reconnaissance and air combat roles for which the CF-104s were not equipped.

Left: The DDH-280 helicopter destroyer, HMCS 'Iroquois', with a CHS-52 Sea King about to land aboard.

Early in 1971 three of the new Tactical Helicopter squadrons were formed – 427 at Petawawa, 430 at Valcartier and 444 at Edmonton; the last of these was subsequently despatched to Lahr in Germany to support the Canadian ground forces element in Europe. There were now 124 new helicopters on order, 50 CUH-1N Iroquois having been added to the requirement so that the existing fleet of 44 miscellaneous small helicopters and Cessnas might be replaced. The first of the Kiowas eventually began arriving in December.

Meanwhile 25 Beechcraft Musketeers, which had been winners of a 1969 contest, were acquired to replace the aging Chipmunks in the primary training role, and eight DHC-6 Twin Otters were ordered to undertake search and rescue; five were to replace a similar number of Dakotas involved in these duties, while one was to replace the lone Caribou still with the UN. A fifth Boeing 707-320C was also ordered to complete replacement of the Yukon in 437 Squadron; two of the new aircraft would be permanently converted as tankers for the Mobile Command CF-5As, the NATO assignment of which could require emergency transfer to Norway or Denmark at any time.

The 434 Squadron at Cold Lake was now acting as Operational Training Squadron for the CF-5A, while the two-seat CF-5D version, 26 of which had been acquired, was now beginning to replace the T-33A-N Silver Stars in the advanced training role; others were replacing the T-33 in coastal water inshore photo-reconnaissance duties.

Toward the end of 1971 it was announced that the two Bomarc squadrons were to be scrapped by September 1972, and that the whole defense of Eastern Canada would then fall on the three Voodoo units. When this happened, and the nuclear role of the CF-104s in Europe ended, the only nuclear weapons left in Canadian service would be the Genie missiles carried by the Voodoos. The Argus, however, would not begin phase-out in 1973 after all, but would be granted a temporary reprieve, as no suitable replacement

was in view. However, 22 surplus CF-104s – 15 single seaters and seven CF-104Ds – were sold to Denmark; 13 more were later to be sold to Norway.

It was soon discovered that the disposal of the Caribou during 1971 had left the CAF short of tactical transports, and early in 1972 the purchase of more Buffalo and Twin Otters was considered, while the 23 C-130s which provided the backbone of the force (19 C-130Es and five C-130Hs) were overhauled and modernized. In the meantime 429 Squadron at Edmonton and 440 at Winnipeg were amalgamated as 440 Transport and Rescue Squadron based at Edmonton with four Buffalo and two Twin Otters, plus a detachment of two more Twin Otters at Yellowknife.

By mid-summer all the new helicopters had been delivered, and two more squadrons had been formed – 408 at Edmonton and 422 at Gagetown – while the Hiller CH-112 Nomads were retired, giving way to the Kiowas. These changes completed the re-equipment program for some time, and the early seventies became a period of reduced flying hours to conserve the lives of the rapidly aging main operational equipment. Only the CF-5As could now be considered even moderately modern; the CF-104s were long overdue for replacement, while despite their recent upgrading the CF-101Fs were no striplings. It was the once so modern Argus which gave the greatest cause for concern, however, as it was by far the longest-serving type still on the inventory, and by the very nature of its duties, had to put in more flying hours than most aircraft. Consequently early in 1973 a contest for a replacement was set in hand, while a Voodoo replacement was also considered. No results transpired, however, and in January 1974 any decision was postponed indefinitely.

Training schedules were, however, modified, 25 Tutors which had been held in store, being returned to service, while five more C-130s were ordered to replace the remaining Dakotas in the Air

Navigation and Instrument Rating School at Winnipeg, which had now taken on the mantle of 429 Squadron.

Some new equipment arrived in January 1975 when eight CH-47 Chinook heavy transport helicopters were delivered to 450 Squadron, while at last after seven years of unified command, it was tacitly admitted that the experiment had failed and integration was reversed, new army, navy and air forces being re-formed in fact, if not in name. Inflation was now biting hard on the Canadian economy, and the Budget, despite guaranteed increases in annual expenditure, was not even retaining its value. In an effort to cut operating costs still further the decision was taken to store 12 of the remaining 56 Voodoos, and retain the squadrons at lower establishment. The number of CF-5As with 433 and 434 Squadrons was also to be cut from 27 to 20, although No 1 FTS was to be allowed to retain its 12 C-5Ds. Argus operational strength was also to be cut from 32 to 26; five squadrons were now operating these aircraft, 449

Above: Backbone of the transport force during the 1950's was the Fairchild C 119 which served with 435 and 436 Squadrons.
Below: DHC-Grumman CS2F-1 Trackers of the RCN shortly before the amalgamation of the Canadian armed forces, aboard the aircraft carrier HMCS 'Bonaventure'.

having been formed as Operational Training Squadron, but one of these was now to be disbanded. Later in the year it was decided to sell 412 Squadron's Dassault Falcons, but this decision was later reversed.

At last a decision was taken regarding the Argus replacement at the start of 1976, 18 modified Lockheed P-3C Orions being ordered as the CP-140 Aurora. These would go to the Greenwood squadrons in the east first – now known as VP 404, 405 and 415; 404 now replaced VP 449 as training unit. In the west VP 407 at Comox would be the last to replace its six Argus with four of the new aircraft. However, it was to be January 1979 before the first Aurora was rolled out from Lockheed's Burbank plant, and more than another year before the first was delivered to the CAF! Meanwhile other anti-submarine patrol duties continued to be undertaken with the ex-RCN aircraft at Shearwater by VP 423 and 443 with 12 and 10 Sea Kings respectively, and VP 880 with 13 Trackers.

The CH-113A Voyageur helicopters that had been released by the Chinooks from 450 Squadron had been converted to the CH-113 Labrador standard for search and rescue, and during 1976 were supplied to 424 Squadron to replace the Twin Otters in this role. Reprieved from sale, three of the Falcons were converted as electronics countermeasures aircraft and were despatched to 414 Squadron at North Bay to augment the old CF-100s and T-33s, while two DHC-7 STOL transports were acquired in 1978 to replace the CC-109 Cosmopolitans which had been in use in Germany for communications since 1960.

By 1979 the question of a new fighter aircraft (NFA) was again being considered as critical. Only 99 CF-104s now remained, and the squadrons in Germany were being maintained at 16, rather than 18 aircraft strength. Some 56 CF-101Fs remained, as did 61 CF-5As – most in store. Initially the list for consideration included all current US types – F-14, F-15, F-16 and F-18; the French Mirage F1 and 2000, and the Panavia Tornado, covetous eyes being cast on the multi-role capabilities of types like the Tornado. However, after initial study, the contenders were narrowed down to the General Dynamics F-16 Falcon and the McDonnell-Douglas F-18 Hornet, some 130-150 examples of the design eventually to be chosen seeming a likely requirement. Months of discussion followed, political, economic and military advantages and disadvantages being weighed up and balanced. During the summer of 1979 attempts were made to acquire Grumman F-14 Tomcats which had been ordered for the Iranian Air Force before the revolution in that country, but in a storm of Middle Eastern protest, this attempt came to naught, and the decision was shelved pending a forthcoming general election.

The election produced a hung parliament, and another followed in the spring of 1980, following which a provisional order was placed with McDonnell-Douglas for 113 CF-18As and 24 two-seat CF-18Bs, the twin-engined configuration of the more expensive Hornet having won the day, when operations over the Canadian wilderness were considered. The order was subject to the US government waiving at least a part of its Research and Development Levy on the order, failure to do which could reduce the order by up to eight aircraft. In the event the full waiver was forthcoming, and the order was confirmed. Fifty-four of the new aircraft are intended for service in Europe, the remaining 83 to be Canadian-based. Once again it had been seen in 1979 that whatever the decision, delivery was likely to be many months away, and a program of refurbishment to the remaining CF-104s was instituted to extend their useful life. The decision to phase out the remaining Dakotas was also reversed, and similar refurbishment was undertaken to extend their life well into the eighties, with six still in service with 429 Squadron, one more as a radar trainer for CF-104 pilots, and two held in store as replacements. During 1980 five CH-113A and six CH-113 helicopters were also upgraded for continued service with the search and rescue units.

Left: A CF-5A, the Canadair-built version of the Northrop F-5A
Freedom Fighter, releases a salvo of rockets.
Top: Mobile Command CF-5A with maximum underwing loads.
Above: The ubiquitous Dassault Fan-Jet Falcon employed first by 412
Squadron for high-speed VIP transport duties.
Below: The powerful McDonnell CF-101B Voodoo.

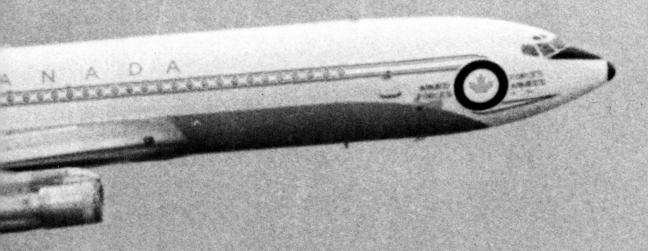

Left: One of the five Boeing 707-320 transports acquired for 437 Squadron, mainly to provide in-flight refuelling capability to the Mobile Force's CF-5A squadrons.
Below: CHS-52 Sea King helicopter.

Left: One of the biggest disappointments for the Canadian forces was the Boeing IM-99B Bomarc nuclear-headed anti-bomber guided missile. Originally intended as the main strength of Air Defence Command, in the event they equipped only two squadrons as back-up to the Voodoo force. Below: Newest equipment for the service is the CF-18 Canadair version of the McDonnell-Douglas F-18 Falcon. Two of the initial batch of CF-18B two-seat conversion aircraft of 410 Operational Training Squadron are seen here in flight from Bagotville.

Early in 1981 new orders were placed for Boeing 737s and six Canadair Challengers, the former to replace the old Cosmopolitans in 412 Squadron, which would themselves then go to 429 Squadron to replace the Dakotas and C-130s as navigation trainers, while the latter would replace the Falcons in 412 and the three in 414 Squadron. Before the year was out the whole order was canceled, however, but in April 1982 it was reinstated in respect of just two of the three 412 Squadron Falcons, which will then be passed on to join those in 414 Squadron. Another 1981 order for Bell 206B Jet Ranger II helicopters was not canceled, these replacing the Kiowas in No 3 FTS. The Kiowas were then delivered to the Air Reserve Wing, and were issued to 400, 401, 411 and 438 Squadrons at Montreal and Toronto.

At last in September 1981 the Aurora entered service with Maritime Command. VP 405 undertook the first operational flights during March after its crews had undergone conversion training

Above: A trio of DHC-6 Twin Otters of 440 (Transport and Rescue) Squadron.
Right: The DHC Buffalo STOL tactical transport was acquired initially as the CC-115, 429 'Bison' Squadron being formed to operate these aircraft.

with the VP 404 operational conversion squadron, and soon VP 415 had also converted to bring Air Group 28 at Greenwood to full strength on the new aircraft. Before the year was out VP 407 in the West had also received the new aircraft.

Plans for the CF-18 program were also advanced, the first aircraft being delivered in October 1982. Initially it was thought that the CF-101 operational training squadron would be disbanded, and that it would be 417 Squadron, the CF-104 OT Squadron, that would introduce the new fighter into service. In the event, however, it was the former unit, 410 Squadron, which received the first aircraft for training and a secondary operational role. With delivery of the CF-18 planned to run at the rate of two per month until 1988, 410 is not due to be fully up to strength until June 1984. During 1982 the order for the CF-18A version of the aircraft was provisionally increased by 11 to 124. Squadrons were due to convert at the rate of two per year, and by 1986 it is planned that most CF-101Fs and CF-104Gs will have been replaced, the CF-5A following during

1987. 409 Squadron is due to become the first operational squadron in June 1984, followed by:

November 1984	425 Squadron
June 1985	439 Squadron
December 1985	421 Squadron
June 1986	441 Squadron
November 1986	433^e Escadrille
June 1987	434 Squadron
November 1987	416 Squadron

When the CF-5As are replaced they will be transferred to a new 419 Tactical Fighter Training Squadron at Cold Lake. At the time of writing, however, there were still no fully-equipped CF-18 squadrons in existence, and the Air Component of the Canadian Armed Forces possessed a strength of some 33 Regular and six Reserve Air Squadrons.

Canadian Forces Europe

No 1 Canadian Air Group

421, 439, 441 Squadrons	CF-104	Baden-Söllingen
444 Squadron	CUH-1N Iroquois	Lahr

Maritime Command
Air Group 28

VP-404, 405, 415	CP-140 Aurora	Greenwood
VP-407	CP-140 Aurora	Comox
VP-423, 443	Sea King	Shearwater
VP-880	Tracker	Shearwater

Mobile Command

433ᵉ Escadrille tactique de combat	CF-5A	Bagotville
434 Operational Training Squadron	CF-5A	Cold Lake
403 Operational Training Squadron	CUH-1N Iroquois	
408 Squadron	CUH-1N Iroquois	Edmonton
422 Squadron	CUH-1N Iroquois	Gagetown
427 Squadron	CUH-1N Iroquois	Petawawa
430 Squadron	CUH-1N Iroquois	Valcartier
450 Squadron	CH-147 Chinook	Namao/Trenton

Air Defense Command

409 Squadron	CF-101F	Comox
416 Squadron	CF-101F	Chatham
425 Squadron	CF-101F	Bagotville
410 Operational Training Squadron	CF-101F/CF-18	Bagotville
417 Operational Training Squadron	CF-104	Cold Lake
414 ECM Squadron	CF-100, T-33, Falcon	Uplands

Air Transport and Training Command

412 Squadron	Falcon, Challenger	
435, 436 Squadrons	C-130	
437 Squadron	Boeing 707-320	
424 Search & Rescue Squadron	CH-113 Labrador	
440 Transport & Rescue Squadron	Buffalo, Twin Otter	Edmonton
429 Air Nav. & Instrument Rating Squadron	C-130, Dakota	Winnipeg
448 Technical Evaluation Squadron		

Air Reserve

401, 438 Squadrons	Kiowa	Montreal
400, 411 Squadrons	Kiowa	Toronto
402 Squadron	Otter	Winnipeg
418 Squadron	Otter	Edmonton

Squadron Code Letters Allocated to RCAF Squadrons, 1946-51

AA	400 Squadron		AQ	414 Squadron
AB	401 Squadron		AS	416 Squadron
AC	402 Squadron		AT	417 Squadron
AD	403 Squadron		AU	418 Squadron
AF	404 Squadron		AW	420 Squadron
AG	405 Squadron		AX	421 Squadron
AK	408 Squadron		BA	424 Squadron
AM	410 Squadron		BQ	438 Squadron
AN	411 Squadron		BU	442 Squadron
AO	412 Squadron		QP	406 Squadron
AP	413 Squadron			

Squadron Code Letters Allocated to RCAF Squadrons, 1951 onwards (discontinued 1960s)

AN	410 Squadron		KE	440 Squadron
AO	412 Squadron		KH	411 Squadron
AP	413 Squadron		LP	409 Squadron
AQ	414 Squadron		MN	408 Squadron
AS	416 Squadron		MP	415 Squadron
AT	417 Squadron		NQ	423 Squadron
AW	420 Squadron		PF	443 Squadron
AX	421 Squadron		PR	403 Squadron
BA	424 Squadron		QT	401 Squadron
BB	425 Squadron, later 427 Squadron		RX	407 Squadron
BD	427 Squadron (later BB)		SA	445 Squadron
BH	430 Squadron		SL	442 Squadron
BQ	438 Squadron		SP	404 Squadron
BT	441 Squadron		SV	402 Squadron
DL	432 Squadron		TF	422 Squadron
FG	433 Squadron		UD	419 Squadron
GW	400 Squadron		VH	444 Squadron
HG	428 Squadron		VN	405 Squadron
HO	418 Squadron		XK	406 Squadron
IG	439 Squadron			

Developed from the Bristol Brittania airliner, the Canadair CP 107 Argus maritime reconnaissance aircraft remained in service for over 20 years. This 405 Squadron machine shows well its clean lines.

Formal and Popular Names Allocated to RCAF Squadrons

400 Squadron	'City of Toronto'	424 Squadron	Tiger
401 Squadron	'City of Westmont'	425 Squadron	Alouette
402 Squadron	'City of Winnipeg'	426 Squadron	Thunderbird
403 Squadron	Wolf/'City of Calgary'	427 Squadron	Lion
404 Squadron	Buffalo	428 Squadron	Ghost
405 Squadron	Eagle/'Vancouver'	429 Squadron	Bison
406 Squadron	Lynx/'City of Saskatoon'	430 Squadron	Silver Falcon
407 Squadron	Demon	431 Squadron	Iroquois
408 Squadron	Goose	432 Squadron	Leaside/Panther
409 Squadron	Crossbow/Nighthawk	433 Squadron	Porcupine
410 Squadron	Cougar	434 Squadron	Bluenose/Bluenose Sailboat
411 Squadron	Bear	435 Squadron	Chinthe
412 Squadron	Falcon	436 Squadron	Elephant
413 Squadron	Elephant/Tusker	437 Squadron	Husky
414 Squadron	Black Knight	438 Squadron	'City of Montreal'
415 Squadron	Swordfish	439 Squadron	Tiger
416 Squadron	Lynx	440 Squadron	No name found
417 Squadron	'City of Windsor'	441 Squadron	Silver Fox
418 Squadron	'City of Edmonton'/Eskimo	442 Squadron	'City of Vancouver'
419 Squadron	Moose	443 Squadron	'City of New Westminster'
420 Squadron	Snowy Owl/'City of London'	444 Squadron	Cobra
421 Squadron	Red Indian	445 Squadron	No name found
422 Squadron	Tomahawk	446-450 Squadrons	No names found
423 Squadron	Bald Eagle		

INDEX

Acknowledgments

The author and the publisher would like to thank David Eldred who designed this book and Ron Watson who compiled the index. Special thanks are due to the Canadian Forces Photographic Unit who supplied nearly all of the photographs, and to Chaz Bowyer who supplied those listed below.

Chaz Bowyer: pages 8 (1), 10 (3), 12 (2).